CROCHET EDGES

MARGARET METCALFE

Kangaroo Press

ACKNOWLEDGMENTS

I wish to thank my husband John and my family for their patience and encouragement, my students for their support and interest in my patterns, and DMC for the use of their cottons.

CROCHET EDGES

First published in Australia in 1999 by Kangaroo Press
An imprint of Simon & Schuster (Australia) Pty Limited
20 Barcoo Street, East Roseville NSW 2069

A Viacom Company
Sydney New York London Toronto Tokyo Singapore

© Margaret Metcalfe 1999

National Library of Australia
Cataloguing-in-Publication data

Metcalfe, Margaret.
Crochet edges.

Includes index.
ISBN 0 86417 931 6.

1. Crocheting - Patterns. I. Title.

746.434041

Cover design: Vivien Valk
Illustrations: Lesley Boston
Photography: Barry Nancarrow Productions Newcastle

Set in Garamond 11/13.2
Printed in Singapore by Colour Symphony Pte Ltd

10 9 8 7 6 5 4 3 2 1

CONTENTS

HINTS ON READING CROCHET PATTERNS

◆ The chain on the hook is never counted as a stitch.

◆ Read the whole pattern before starting. If you are unsure of any part of the pattern, practice that section before starting the article. It would be silly to start a pattern that you don't understand.

◆ Read each row before starting it.

◆ Mark off each row of the pattern as you work—this way you won't lose your place

◆ Always insert the hook *from front to back* unless the pattern states otherwise.

◆ Always insert hook *under* the top two loops unless the pattern states otherwise.

◆ There should be only one loop left on the hook at the completion of each stitch or sequence.

◆ Always work *into* the turning chain unless the pattern states otherwise.

◆ An asterisk * means 'work the instructions following the *' as many times as specified.

◆ Parenthesis brackets ( ) mean 'work the instructions in the brackets' as many times as specified.

◆ *Rep* or *repeat* means 'work the instructions the number of times specified'; for example, 'rep 5 times' means 'do the instructions 6 times' (one for the original and 5 for the repeats)—remember, you can't repeat something until you have already done it.

◆ If the pattern states 'work 5 times' this means 'do that instruction only 5 times'.

◆ *Rows*: Rows are usually for straight crochet without curves; you turn the work at the end of each row unless the pattern states otherwise.

◆ *Rounds*: Rounds are used in doilies and any part of a pattern that needs circular or curved work. Most join with a sl st where stated in the pattern. You do not turn the work unless the pattern states otherwise.

◆ *Clusters*: These are usually a series of stitches worked either in the same place or over a number of stitches, and worked off together. The instructions for clusters vary from pattern to pattern. The abbreviation and instructions for each cluster should appear in the abbreviation section of the pattern book or at the beginning of the pattern.

◆ *Beginning cluster*: This is the cluster made at the beginning of a row or round, and will have one less loop than the other clusters in the pattern, because the chain made at the beginning of the row will be the first stitch of the cluster.

◆ *Turning chain*: This is the chain made at the beginning or end of row. If made at the beginning of a row it will be the first stitch, unless the pattern states otherwise. If made at the end of a row it will be the first stitch of the next row after you turn your work, unless the pattern states otherwise.

◆ Turning chains should be worked into; for example, if the pattern says '1tr in turning ch', it means 'work a treble in the last chain made (the turning chain)'.

◆ *Crochet hooks*: Hook sizes quoted are a guide only, you should use the hook you require to achieve the best results. Where a tension is quoted use the hook required to achieve that tension.

◆ *Crochet cotton*: Crochet cottons vary from brand to brand. The quantities given are a guide only and may vary depending on the cotton used, and may also vary from crocheter to crocheter.

◆ *Equivalent crochet terms:*

Australia/Europe		America
ch (chain)	=	ch (chain)
sl st (slip stitch	=	sl st (slip stitch)
dc (double crochet)	=	sc (single crochet)
tr (treble)	=	dc (double crochet)
dtr (double treble)	=	tr (treble)

◆ *Crochet hook equivalents:*

Metric (mm)	Imperial	American
2.0	14	B/1
2.5	12	C/2
3.0	10	D/3
3.5	9	E/4
4.0	8	F/5
4.5	7	G/6
5.0	6	H/8
5.5	5	I/9
6.0	4	J/10
7.0	2	—

HEMMING

Hemstitching This method of sewing is used to make holes in the fabric being edged for the crochet hook to fit through easily. When you buy a handkerchief with holes all the way around the edge it has been hemstitched. A special machine is required for hemstitching. Some craft stores will get articles hemstitched for you at a minimal price. A wing needle can be used on most sewing machines to make the holes, but this is not as successful as hemstitching.

Hint When making a crochet edge to sew on fabric that must be hemmed, make the crocheted edge before you hem the fabric. This way you can cut and hem the fabric to suit the crocheted edge.

Hand sew a crocheted edge to the fabric, as machine sewing has a tendency to stretch the edging.

ABBREVIATIONS

ch chain
dc double crochet
tr treble
htr half treble
dtr double treble
sl st slip stitch
rep repeat
beg beginning
sp space

HOW EACH STITCH IS WORKED

Chain (ch) With a loop on the hook, yoh (yarn over hook) and draw thread through this loop, continue this until required number of chains are made.

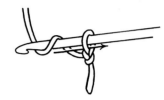

Step 1: Make a slip knot, yoh and pull through a loop

Step 2: Slip knot

Step 3: yoh and draw yarn through loop

1st chain from hook
2nd chain from hook
3rd chain from hook
4th chain from hook
5th chain from hook

Step 4: Continue as step 3 until required number of chain have been made

Step 5: How to count the chain

Double crochet (dc) Make the number of chain required, insert the hook where stated in the pattern, yoh (yarn over hook) and draw through work (there should be 2 loops left on the hook), yoh and draw through both loops on hook (1dc made).

Step 1: Insert hook into 2nd ch from hook, or where stated in pattern

Step 2: yoh and draw a loop through (there should be 2 loops left on hook)

Step 3: yoh and draw through 2 loops on the hook (there should be 1 loop left on hook)

Step 4: Insert hook where stated in pattern and repeat steps 2 and 3

Slip stitch (sl st) Insert hook where stated in pattern, yoh (yarn over hook) and draw through all loops on hook (there should be 1 loop left on hook).

Treble (tr) yoh (yarn over hook) insert hook where stated in pattern, yoh and draw through work, (there should be 3 loops left on hook) yoh and draw through two loops on hook (there should be 2 loops left on hook) yoh and draw through two remaining loops (1tr made).

Step 1: *yoh, insert hook into 4th ch from hook, or where stated in pattern*

Step 2: *yoh and draw through (there should be 3 loops on hook)*

Step 3: *yoh and draw through 2 loops on hook (there should be 2 loops left on hook)*

Step 4: *yoh and draw through 2 loops on hook (there should be 1 loop left on hook)*

Step 5: *yoh and insert hook into next ch, or where stated in pattern, then repeat from step 2*

Half treble (htr) Make the number of chain required, yoh (yarn over hook), insert hook where stated in pattern, yoh and draw through (there should be 3 loops on hook), yoh and draw through all 3 loops on hook (1htr made).

Step 1: *yoh and insert hook into 3rd ch from hook, or where stated in pattern*

Step 2: *yoh and draw through (there should be 3 loops on hook)*

Step 3: *yoh and draw through all 3 loops (there should be 1 loop left on hook), yoh and insert hook in next ch, or where stated in pattern, and repeat steps 2 and 3*

Double treble (dtr) Make the number of chain required, yoh (yarn over hook) twice, insert hook where stated in pattern, yoh and draw through (4 loops on hook), yoh and draw through 2 loops on hook (there should be 3 loops left on hook), yoh and draw through 2 loops on hook (there should be 2 loops left on hook), yoh and draw through 2 remaining loops (1dtr made).

Step 1: *yoh twice, insert hook into 5th ch from hook*

Step 2: *yoh and draw through (there should be 4 loops left on hook)*

Step 3: *yoh and draw through 2 loops (there should be 3 loops left on hook)*

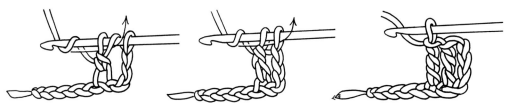

Step 4: *yoh and draw through 2 loops (there should be 2 loops left on hook)*

Step 5: *yoh and draw through 2 loops (there should be only 1 loop left on hook)*

Step 6: *yoh twice, insert hook into next ch, or where stated in pattern, and repeat from step 2*

FACE WASHERS

ADD A TOUCH OF CLASS TO YOUR BATHROOM.

TRIM NOT JUST FACE WASHERS BUT TOWELS AND HANDTOWELS WITH THESE PRETTY EDGES.

GUIDE TO WORKING DOUBLE CROCHET

The first seven face washer edges each begin with a round of double crochet. Maintaining a constant distance between the double crochets is important to keep the work flat and even.

If the double crochets are too close together, the work will look frilly when finished.

If the double crochets are too far apart, the work will pull when finished. Use the following as a guide:

✦ *4-ply cotton:* 10dc to 4 cm (1½") on the sides, and 10dc to 3 cm (1⅛") when working around the corners.

✦ *No 10 cotton:* 12dc to 4 cm (1½") on the sides, and 12dc to 3 cm (1⅛") when working around the corners.

EDGE 1

Materials

1 face washer

50 g DMC Hermina 4-ply cotton (this quantity will make edges for at least six 28 cm [11"] square face washers)

1.75 mm and 2.00 mm crochet hooks

1st round: Using 1.75 mm crochet hook, right side facing, insert hook into the edge, holding cotton at back of work, yoh and draw a loop through, make 1ch (this will be the first dc), make an even number of dc all around the face washer, working them closer together around the corners so that the work doesn't pucker, join with a sl st in first dc made.

Change to 2.00 mm crochet hook.

2nd round: 1dc in same place as 4ch, miss 1dc, *1dc in next dc, 4ch, miss 1dc, rep from * until all sides have been worked, join with a sl st in first dc made.

3rd round: sl st into first 4ch loop, (1dc, 3ch, 1dc) into same loop as the sl st, *(1dc, 3ch, 1dc) into next 4ch loop, rep from * to end, join with a sl st in first dc made. Fasten off.

EDGE 2

Materials

50 g DMC Hermina 4-ply crochet cotton (this quantity will make edges for at least four 28 cm [11"] square face washers)

1 face washer

1.75 mm and 2.00 mm crochet hooks

Note: This is a 4-stitch pattern. If you need more dc than the pattern states, add in multiples of 4 to each side. If less dc are needed, reduce by multiples of 4 on each side.

1st round: With right side facing, and 1.75 mm crochet hook, start in the centre of any corner and make 60dc to centre of next corner, *place a marker in the 60th dc (this will save counting from the beginning all the time), then work 60dc from this marker to the centre of the next corner, rep from * until all sides have been worked, join with a sl st in first dc made.

Change to 2.00 mm crochet hook.

2nd round: 1dc in same place as sl st, miss 1dc, (3tr, 2ch, 3tr) in next dc, miss 1dc, *1dc in next dc, miss 1dc, (3tr, 2ch, 3tr) in next dc, miss 1dc, rep from * to end, join with a sl st in first dc made.

Fasten off.

Edge 3

Materials

1 face washer

50 g DMC Hermina 4-ply cotton (this quantity will make edges for at least four 28 cm [11"] square face washers)

1.75 mm and 2.00 mm crochet hooks

1st round: Right side facing, use 1.75 mm crochet hook, or hook that will work through the washer with ease, work an even number of dc around the washer, working closer together around the corners, join with a sl st in first dc made. *Change to 2.00 mm crochet hook.*

2nd round: 5ch, 1tr in same place as sl st, miss 1dc, *(1tr, 2ch, 1tr) in next dc, miss 1dc, rep from * to end , join with a sl st in 3rd of 5ch made at beg.

3rd round: *(3dc, 3ch, sl st in first ch made) in next 2ch sp, rep from * to end, join with a sl st in first dc.

Fasten off.

Edge 4

Materials

Face washer

50 g DMC Hermina 4-ply cotton (this quantity will make edges for at least five 28 cm [11"] square face washers)

1.75 mm and 2.00 mm crochet hooks

Note: This is a 5-stitch pattern. If you need more dc than the pattern states, add in multiples of 5 to each side. If less dc are needed, reduce by multiples of 5 on each side.

1st round: With right side facing, and 1.75 mm crochet hook, start in the centre of any corner and make 60dc to the centre of next corner, *place a marker in the 60th dc (this will save counting from the beginning all the time), then work 60dc from this marker to the centre of the next corner, rep from * until all sides have been worked, join with a sl st in first dc made.

Change to 2.00 mm crochet hook.

2nd round: 1dc in same place as sl st, *2ch, miss 1dc, 2tr in next dc, 3ch, sl st in top of last tr, 2tr in next dc, 2ch, miss 1dc, 1dc in next dc, rep from * to end , omitting the dc at end of last rep, join with a sl st in first dc made.
Fasten off.

EDGE 5

Materials
1 face washer
50 g DMC Hermina 4-ply cotton (this quantity will make edges for at least four 28 cm [11"] square face washers)
1.75 mm and 2.00 mm crochet hooks

1st round: Right side facing, use 1.75 mm crochet hook, or hook that will work through the washer with ease, work dc evenly around the face washer, to end up with a number of dc divisible by 4, join with a sl st in first dc made.
Change to 2.00 mm crochet hook.
2nd round: 4ch, 1tr in same place as sl st, *miss 1dc, (1tr, 1ch, 1tr) in next dc, rep from * to end, join with a sl st in 3rd of 4ch made at beg.
3rd round: sl st in first 1ch sp, 1dc in same sp, *(3tr, 3ch, sl st in top of last tr made, 3tr) in next 1ch sp, 1dc in next 1ch sp, rep from * to end, omitting dc at end of last rep, join with a sl st in first dc made.
Fasten off.

EDGE 6

This edge is quick to do—only one round.

Materials

Teatowel or face washer

50 g DMC Hermina 4-ply crochet cotton (this quantity will edge three average
 size teatowels or four 28 cm [11"] square face washers)

1.75 mm crochet hook

Insert hook into edge of item to be worked, yoh and draw cotton through, make
2ch, 1dc in same place as join, *4ch, 2tr in last dc, miss the length of the stitch,
1dc in edge, 1dc in same place as last dc, rep from * all around, working closer
together around the corners if necessary to keep the work flat, join with a sl st in
first dc made.

Fasten off.

EDGE 7

*This pattern has only one round, and is pretty when only a
little edge is required. Try it on a teatowel or face washer.*

Materials

1 teatowel or face washer evenly hemmed all around

50 g DMC Hermina 4-ply crochet cotton (this quantity will edge three average size teatowels or five 28 cm {11"] square face washers)

1.75 mm crochet hook, or hook that will go through teatowel fabric with ease

Insert hook into edge over hem, yoh and draw a loop through, make 3ch, 1tr in same place as the join, 3ch, 1tr in top of last tr, 2tr in same place as join, miss about 1 cm (³/₈"), *(2tr, 3ch, 1tr in top of last tr, 2tr) all in same place, miss about 1 cm (³/₈"), rep from * all around, working closer around the corner if required to keep work flat, join with a sl st in 3rd of 3ch made at the beg.
Fasten off.

The edges in this next group are worked with chain and double crochet. The distance the chains are worked apart is important to keep the work flat and even. If the chains are too close the work will look frilly. If the chains are too far apart the work will pull.

For the best results use this guide:

4-PLY COTTON

◆ *5ch loops:* 5 loops to 7 cm (2¾") on the sides, and 4 loops to 4 cm (1½") around the corners.

◆ *4ch loops:* 5 loops to 5 cm (2") on sides, and 4 loops to 3 cm (1¹/₈") around the corners.

◆ *3ch loops:* 5 loops to 4 cm (1½") on sides, and 5 loops to 3 cm (1¹/₈") around the corners.

NO 10 COTTON

◆ *5ch loops:* 5 loops to 6 cm (2³/₈") on sides, and 4 loops to 3 cm (1¹/₈") around corners.

◆ *4ch loops:* 5 loops to 4 cm (1½") on sides, and 4 loops to 2.5 cm (1") around corners

◆ *3ch loops:* 5 loops to 3 cm (1¹/₈") on sides, and 4 loops to 2 cm around corners.

OTHER COTTONS

◆ A pattern using cotton of another ply will tell you how far apart the loops should be, usually the length of the chain between the double crochet.

Edge 8

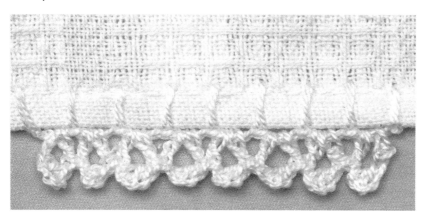

Materials

1 face washer or teatowel
50 g DMC Hermina 4-ply crochet cotton (this quantity will make three teatowels or four face washers)
1.75 mm and 2.00 mm crochet hooks

Note: Work loops closer together around the corners in the first round.

1st round: Right side facing, use 1.75 mm crochet hook, or hook that will work through the item to be worked with ease, insert hook into edge, make 1ch (this will be the first dc), *3ch, miss the length of the 3ch, 1dc, rep from * all around to the end, omitting the dc at end of last rep, join with a sl st in first dc made. *Change to 2.00 mm crochet hook.*

2nd round: sl st into first 3ch loop, (6ch, 1tr in 3rd of 6ch, 1tr) in same loop, *(1tr, 3ch, 1tr in 3rd of 3ch, 1tr) in next 3ch loop, rep from * to end, join with a sl st in 3rd of 6ch made at beg.
Fasten off.

Edge 9

Materials

Face washer
50 g DMC Hermina 4-ply crochet cotton (this quantity will edge four washers)
1.75 mm and 2.00 mm crochet hooks

1st round: With 1.75 mm crochet hook and right side facing, insert hook into face washer, yoh and draw a loop through, make 1ch (this will be the first dc), *4ch, miss the length of the 4ch, 1dc into face washer, rep from * to end, omitting the dc at the end of last rep, join with a sl st in first dc made.
Change to 2.00 mm crochet hook

2nd round: sl st in first 4ch loop, 2dc in same loop as sl st, (3ch, 1dc in last dc made), 3 times, 2dc in same 4ch loop, *2dc in next 4ch loop, (3ch, 1dc in last dc made) 3 times, 2dc in same 4ch loop, rep from * to end, join with a sl st in first dc made.
Fasten off.

DON'T KNOW WHAT TO DO WITH ALL THOSE ENDS OF COTTON?
THE NEXT TWO PATTERNS SHOW YOU HOW TO USE THEM TO ADD A TOUCH OF
COLOUR TO THE BATHROOM.

EDGE 10—TWO-COLOUR

Materials

Quantities of cotton needed will vary depending on the size of the item you are
   working—for an average 28 cm (11") square face washer 50 g DMC Hermina
   4-ply main colour and about 10 g DMC Hermina contrast colour will make
   approximately three edgings
1.75 mm and 2.00 mm crochet hooks

Note: Work closer together around the corners on the first round so that the
work doesn't pucker.

1st round: Right side facing, and using main colour and 1.75 mm crochet hook,
or hook that will fit through the item with ease, insert hook into edge of the
washer, yoh and draw cotton through, make 1ch (this will be counted as first dc),
*5ch, miss the length of the 5ch, 1dc into edge, rep from * evenly around the
item, omitting the dc at end of last rep, join with a sl st. in first dc made.

Change to 2.00 mm crochet hook.

2nd round: sl st in first 5ch loop, 3ch, 1tr, 2ch, 2tr, in same 5ch loop, *(2tr, 2ch, 2tr) in next 5ch loop, rep from * to end, join with a sl st in 3rd of 3ch made at beg. Fasten off main colour.

3rd round: With contrast colour join in same place as sl st, 1dc in same place as join, 1dc in next tr, 1dc in 2ch sp, 3ch, sl st in last dc made, 1dc in same 2ch sp, *1dc in each of next 4tr, (1dc in next 2ch sp, 3ch, sl st in last dc made, 1dc in same 2ch sp), rep from * to last 2tr, 1dc in each of next 2tr, join with a sl st in first dc made. Fasten off.

EDGE 11—TWO-COLOUR

Materials
Face washer
50 g DMC Hermina 4-ply crochet cotton in main colour
30 g DMC Hermina 4-ply crochet cotton in contrast colour (this quantity will make edgings for four face washers)
1.75 mm and 2.00 mm crochet hooks

Note: Work loops closer together around the corners on the first round.

1st round: With main colour and 1.75 mm crochet hook, right side facing, insert hook into item to be worked, yoh and draw a loop through, make 1ch (this will be the first dc), *4ch, miss the length of the 4ch, 1dc, rep from * to end, join with a sl st in first dc made.
Change to 2.00 mm crochet hook.
2nd round: sl st in first 4ch loop, 3ch, 1tr, 2ch, 2tr in same 4ch loop, *(2tr, 2ch, 2tr) in next 4ch loop, rep from * to end, join with a sl st in 3rd of 3ch made at beg. Fasten off main colour.

3rd round: Join contrast in any 2ch sp, 1dc in same sp, *5ch, 1dc in next 2ch sp, rep from * to end, omitting the dc at the end of last rep, join with a sl st in first dc made.
4th round: *(3dc in next 5ch loop, 3ch, sl st in last dc made, 2dc in same 5ch loop), rep from * to end, join with a sl st in first dc made. Fasten off.

FOR THE KITCHEN

*Still don't know what to do with all those ends of cotton?
The following patterns show you how to use them, as well as adding
a touch of class and colour to the humble teatowel.*

Two-colour teatowel I

Materials
Teatowel or face washer
50 g DMC Hermina 4-ply crochet cotton in main colour
10 g DMC Hermina 4-ply contrast colour for each item
1.75 mm and 2.00 mm crochet hooks

Note: Work loops closer together around the corners on the first round.

1st round: Start anywhere, with right side facing, and using main colour and 1.75 mm crochet hook, or hook that will fit through the fabric with ease, insert hook into the edge over the hem, yoh and draw cotton through, make 1ch (this will be counted as the first dc), *5ch, miss the length of the 5ch, 1dc, rep from * evenly around the teatowel or washer, omitting the dc at the end of last rep, join with a sl st in first dc.
Change to 2.00 mm crochet hook.
2nd round: sl st into first 5ch loop, (4ch, 1tr, 1ch, 1tr, 1ch, 1tr) in same loop, *(1tr, 1ch, 1tr, 1ch, 1tr, 1ch, 1tr) in next 5ch loop, rep from * to end, join with a sl st in 3rd of 4ch made at beg. Fasten off main colour.
3rd round: With contrast colour join cotton in first 1ch space after the sl st, 1dc in same space, *(1dc, 3ch, 1dc, 5ch, 1dc, 3ch, 1dc) in next 1ch space, 1dc in each of next two 1ch spaces, rep from * to end, omitting 1dc at the end of last rep, join with a sl st in first dc made.
Fasten off.

THREE-COLOUR TEATOWEL

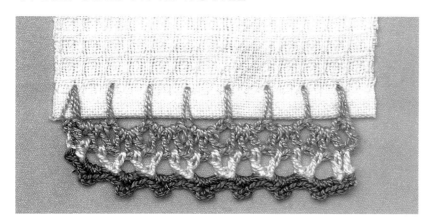

Materials

Teatowel with hems no wider than 1 cm ($^3/_8$")

Small quantities of cotton in three colours (amounts will vary depending on the size of the teatowel and ply of cotton used)

1.50 mm crochet hook for DMC Maeva No 10 cotton, 1.75 mm crochet hook for DMC Hermina 4-ply cotton, or hook to work through the teatowel with ease for 1st row, changing to right sized hook for 2nd row

Note: Work both ends the same, having the same number of loops on each end.

1st row: Right side facing, using 1st colour, work along the short end of teatowel, insert hook close to edge over the hem (you may have to use a smaller hook for first 2dc, and last 2dc), yoh and draw cotton through, make 1ch (this will be counted as the first dc), 1dc in same place as last dc, *5ch, miss the length of the 5ch, 1dc, rep from * to end of short end, 1dc in same place as last dc, turn.

2nd row: 3ch, *(1tr, 1ch, 1tr, 1ch, 1tr) in next 5ch loop, rep from * to end, 1tr in last dc, fasten off.

3rd row: With 2nd colour and right side facing, join in top of first tr, 3ch, *1tr in next 1ch sp, 3ch, 1tr in next 1ch sp, rep from * to end, 1tr in 3rd of 3ch, fasten off.

4th row: With 3rd colour, and right side facing, join in top of first tr, 1dc in same place as join, *(2dc, 3ch, 2dc) in next 3ch sp, rep from * to end, 1dc in last tr. Fasten off.

Work other end.

TWO-COLOUR TEATOWEL II

Materials

Small quantities of two colours (amounts will vary depending on the size of the
teatowel and ply of cotton used)
1.50 mm crochet hook for DMC Maeva No 10 cotton, 1.75 mm crochet hook for
DMC Hermina 4-ply cotton, or hook to work through the teatowel with ease
for 1st row, change to right sized hook for 2nd row

Note: Work both ends the same, having the same number of loops on each end.

1st row : Right side facing, using 1st colour, work along the short end of teatowel,
insert hook close to edge over the hem (you may have to use a smaller hook for
first 2dc, and last 2dc), yoh and draw cotton through, make 1ch (this will be
counted as the first dc), 1dc in same place as last dc, *5ch, miss the length of the
5ch, 1dc, rep from * to end of short end, 1dc in same place as last dc, turn.
2nd row: 3ch, *(1tr, 1ch, 1tr, 1ch, 1tr) in next 5ch loop, rep from * to end, 1tr in
last dc, fasten off.
3rd row: With 2nd colour and right side facing, join cotton in first tr, 1dc in same
place as the join, *1dc in next 1ch sp, 3ch, 1dc in next tr, 3ch, 1dc in next 1ch sp,
rep from * to last 2 tr, miss 1tr, 1dc in last tr.
Fasten off.

TEATOWEL HANDTOWEL

This pattern is for a teatowel 49 cm (19") wide.

Materials

1 towelling teatowel cut in half and hemmed so that all edges are even
50 g DMC Hermina 4-ply crochet cotton (50 g will make three edges)
1.75 mm and 2.00 mm crochet hooks
1 button

With right side facing, work top first. Divide edge of fabric into four, place a
marker (safety pin or cotton) in each quarter.
Using 1.75 mm crochet hook work as follows:

1st row: Make 97dc evenly across the top edge of teatowel, working 24dc in each of first three quarters, and 25dc in last quarter, turn.

2nd row: *Change to 2.00 mm crochet hook,* 3ch, *1tr in next dc, rep from * to end, (97tr counting the 3ch as 1tr), turn.

3rd row: 3ch, miss next 2tr, *1tr in next tr, 1ch, miss next 2tr, rep from * to end, working the last tr in 3rd of 3ch, turn.

4th row: 3ch, *1tr in 1ch sp, 1tr in next tr, rep from * to end, 1tr in 3rd of 3ch, turn.

5th row: 3ch, miss next 2tr, 1tr in next tr, *1ch, miss next 2tr, 1tr in next tr, rep from * to end, working last tr in 3rd of 3ch, turn.

6th row: 3ch, *1tr in 1ch sp, 1tr in next tr, rep from * to end, 1tr in 3rd of 3ch, turn.

7th row: 3ch, miss next 2tr, 1tr in next tr, *1ch, miss next 2tr, 1tr in next tr, rep from * to last tr and 3ch, 1ch, miss 1tr, 1tr in 3rd of 3ch, turn.

8th row: 3ch, *1tr in 1ch sp, 1tr in next tr, rep from * to end, 1tr in 3rd of 3ch, turn.

9th row: 3ch, miss next 2tr, 1tr in next tr, *1ch, miss next 2tr, 1tr in next tr, rep from * to end, working last tr in 3rd of 3ch, turn.

10th row: 3ch, *1tr in 1ch sp, 1tr in next tr, rep form * to end, 1tr in 3rd of 3ch, turn.

11th row: 3ch, miss next tr, 1tr in next tr, *1ch, miss next 2tr, 1tr in next tr, rep from * to end, working last tr in 3rd of 3ch, turn.

12th row: 3ch, *1tr in 1ch sp, 1tr in next tr, rep from * to end, 1tr in 3rd of 3ch, turn.

13th row: 3ch, miss next tr, 1tr in each of next 8tr, miss next tr, 1tr in 3rd of 3ch, turn.

14th row: 3ch, 1tr in each of next 8tr, 1tr in 3rd of 3ch, turn.

Rep 14th row 8 times.

Next row: 3ch, 1tr in each of next 2tr, 4ch, miss 4tr, 1tr in each of next 2tr, 1tr in 3rd of 3ch, turn.

Next row: 3ch, 1tr in each of next 2tr, 4tr in 4ch loop, 1tr in each of next 2tr, 1tr in 3rd of 3ch, turn.

Change to 1.75 mm crochet hook.

Border: With right side facing, working all of the teatowel, proceed as follows: 1dc in work, 3ch, 1tr in last dc made, miss the length of the stitch, 1dc in work, *3ch, 1tr in last dc made, miss the length of the stitch, 1dc in work, rep from * working into crochet work and all sides of towel to end, omitting the 1dc at end of last rep, join with a sl st in first dc made.

Fasten off.

Sew button on right side of 14th row.

PINEAPPLE-TOPPED KITCHEN TOWEL

This towel top can be made in one or two colours.

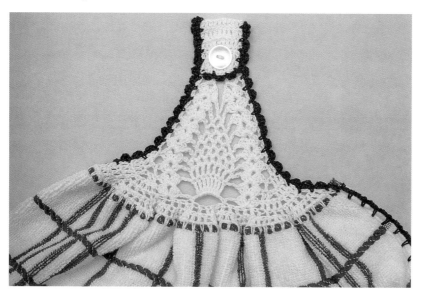

Materials
1 towelling teatowel cut in half and hemmed, or top and bottom evenly overlocked
50 g DMC Hermina 4-ply cotton (this quantity will edge three towels)
10 g DMC Hermina 4-ply cotton contrast colour (if required)
1.75 mm and 2.00 mm crochet hooks
1 button

With right side facing, work top first. Place a marker (safety pin or length of cotton) at mid-point.

1st row: With 1.75 mm crochet hook and main colour, insert hook into top of towel, yoh and draw cotton through, make 1ch (this will be the first dc), *1ch, 1dc, rep from * 30 times to halfway marker, then rep from first * 32 times to end (there should be 65dc), remove marker, turn.

Change to 2.00 mm crochet hook.

2nd row: 3ch, *1tr in next 1ch sp, rep from * to end (65tr, counting the 3ch as 1tr), turn.

3rd row: 3ch, *miss 1tr, 1tr in next tr, rep from * to end, work last tr in 3rd of 3ch (33tr, counting the 3ch as 1tr), turn.

4th row: 3ch, 1tr in each of next 3tr, miss 1tr, 1tr in each of next 4tr, miss 1tr, (3tr, 2ch, 3tr) in next tr, 3ch, miss 2tr, 1dc in next tr, 7ch, miss 5tr, 1dc in next tr, 3ch, miss 2tr, (3tr, 2ch, 3tr) in next tr, miss 1tr, 1tr in each of next 4tr, miss 1tr, 1tr in each of next 3tr, 1tr in 3rd of 3ch, turn.

5th row: 3ch, 1tr in each of next 3tr, miss 2tr, 1tr in each of next 2tr, (3tr, 2ch, 3tr) in next 2ch sp, 3ch, 8dtr in 7ch loop, 3ch, (3tr, 2ch, 3tr) in next 2ch sp, miss 3tr, 1tr in each of next 2tr, miss 2tr, 1tr in each of next 3tr, 1tr in 3rd of 3ch, turn.

6th row: 3ch, 1tr in each of next 2tr, miss 2tr, 1tr in next tr, (3tr, 2ch, 3tr) in next 2ch sp, 3ch, *1tr in next dtr, 1ch, rep from * 6 times, 1tr in last dtr, 3ch, (3tr, 2ch, 3tr) in next 2ch sp, miss 3tr, 1tr in next tr, miss 2tr, 1tr in each of next 2tr, 1tr in 3rd of 3ch, turn.

7th row: 3ch, 1tr in next tr, (3tr, 2ch, 3tr) in next 2ch sp, *3ch, 1dc in next 1ch sp, rep from * 6 times, 3ch, (3tr, 2ch, 3tr) in next 2ch sp, miss 5tr, 1tr in next tr, 1tr in 3rd of 3ch, turn.

8th row: 3ch, (3tr, 2ch, 3tr) in 2ch sp, 3ch, miss 3ch, *1dc in next 3ch sp, 3ch, rep from * 5 times, (3tr, 2ch, 3tr) in next 2ch sp, 1tr in 3rd of 3ch, turn.

9th row: 3ch, (3tr, 2ch, 3tr) in 2ch sp, 3ch, miss 3ch, *1dc in next 3ch sp, 3ch, rep from * 4 times, (3tr, 2ch, 3tr) in next 2ch sp, 1tr in 3rd of 3ch, turn.

10th row: 3ch, (3tr, 2ch, 3tr) in next 2ch sp, 3ch, miss 3ch, *1dc in next 3ch sp, 3ch, rep from * 3 times (3tr, 2ch, 3tr) in next 2ch sp, 1tr in 3rd of 3ch, turn.

11th row: 3ch, (3tr, 2ch, 3tr) in next 2ch sp, 3ch, miss 3ch, *1dc in next 3ch sp, 3ch, rep from * twice, (3tr, 2ch, 3tr) in next 2ch sp, 1tr in 3rd of 3ch, turn.

12th row: 3ch, (3tr, 2ch, 3tr) in next 2ch sp, 3ch, miss 3ch, *1dc in next 3ch sp, 3ch, rep from * once, (3tr, 2ch, 3tr) in next 2ch sp, 1tr in 3rd of 3ch, turn.

13th row: 3ch, (3tr, 2ch, 3tr) in next 2ch sp, 3ch, miss 3ch, 1dc in next 3ch sp, 3ch, (3tr, 2ch, 3tr) in next 3ch sp, 1tr in 3rd of 3ch , turn.

14th row: 3ch, (4tr in next 2ch space) twice, 1tr in 3rd of 3ch, turn.

15th row: 3ch, 1tr in each of next 8 tr, 1tr in 3rd of 3ch, turn.

Rep 15th row 8 times.

Next row: 3ch, 1tr in each of next 2tr, 3ch, miss 4tr, 1tr in each of next 2tr, 1tr in 3rd of 3ch, turn.

Next row: 3ch, 1tr in each of next 2tr, 4tr in next 3ch sp, 1tr in each of next 2tr, 1tr in 3rd of 3ch, fasten off.

Border: With right side facing, main colour or contrast and 1.75 mm crochet hook, proceed as follows, starting at bottom of towel: insert hook into edge, yoh and draw cotton through, make 1ch (this will be the first dc), 4ch, 1tr in 1st of 4ch, miss the length of the stitch, 1dc in work, *3ch, 1tr in last dc made, miss the length of the stitch, 1dc in work, rep from * all around the towel, working evenly around the crochet work, join with a sl st in first dc made.

Sew button on right side of 14th row.

SHELL HALF-TOWEL HANDTOWEL

This pattern has been written for a teatowel 49 cm (19") wide.

Materials

1 towelling teatowel cut in half and hemmed or overlocked, so that all edges are
    even
50 g DMC Hermina 4-ply cotton (this quantity will make two)
10 g DMC Hermina 4-ply cotton contrast colour if required
1.75 mm and 2.00 mm crochet hooks
1 button

Special abbreviation
shell = (3tr, 2ch, 3tr)

With right side facing, work top first, divide top into four, place a marker in each
quarter.
Using 1.75 mm crochet hook work as follows:
1st row: Make 97dc evenly across the top edge of the towel, working 24dc in
each of first three quarters, and 25dc in last quarter, remove markers.
Change to 2.00 mm crochet hook.
2nd row: 3ch, 1tr in each of next 11dc, *miss 2dc, shell in next dc, miss 2dc, 1tr
in each of next 12dc, rep from * to end.
3rd row: 3ch, miss 1tr, 1tr in each of next 9tr, *shell in 2ch space of next shell,
miss 1tr, 1tr in each of next 10tr, rep from * to end.
4th row: 3ch, miss 1tr, 1tr in each of next 7tr, *shell in 2ch space of shell, miss
1tr, 1tr in each of next 8tr, rep from * to end.
5th row: 3ch, miss 1tr, 1tr in each of next 5tr, *shell in 2ch space of shell, miss
1tr, 1tr in each of next 6tr, rep from * to end.
6th row: 3ch, miss 1tr, 1tr in each of next 3tr, *shell in 2ch space of shell, miss
1tr, 1tr in each of next 4tr, rep from * to end.
7th row: 3ch, miss 1tr, 1tr in next tr, *shell in 2ch space of shell, miss 1tr, 1tr in
each of next 2tr, rep from * to end.
8th row: 3ch, *shell in 2ch space of shell, rep from * to end, 1tr in 3rd of 3ch.
9th row: 3ch, *4tr in 2ch space of shell, rep from * to end, 1tr in 3rd of 3ch.
10th row: 3ch, miss 1tr, *1tr in each of next 2tr, miss 2tr, rep from * to end, 1tr
in 3rd of 3ch.
11th row: 3ch, miss next tr, 1tr in each of next 8tr, 1tr in 3rd of 3ch.
12th row: 3ch, 1tr in each of next 8tr, 1tr in 3rd of 3ch.
Rep 12th row 8 times.
21st row: 3ch, 1tr in each of next 2tr, 4ch, miss 4tr, 1tr in each of next 2tr, 1tr in
3rd of 3ch.
22nd row: 3ch, 1tr in each of next 2tr, 4tr in 4ch loop, 1tr in each of next 2tr, 1tr
in 3rd of 3ch.
Border: Right side facing, working all around the towel and crochet work, make
border as follows: 1dc in edge, 3ch, 1tr in last dc made, *miss the length of the
stitch, 1dc in towel or crochet work, 3ch, 1tr in last dc made, rep from * to end,
join with a sl st in first dc made.
Fasten off.
Sew button on 12th row.

Variation: Use contrast colour for border.

Face washer edges: from left to right, Edge 1 (page 9), Edge 2 (page 10) and Edge 3 (page 11)

Face washer edges: clockwise from left, Edge 4 (page 11), Edge 5 (page 12), Edge 6 (page 13) and Edge 7 (page 13)

Face washer edges: clockwise from centre left, Two-colour Edge 10 (page 16), Two-colour Edge 11 (page 17), Edge 9 (page 15), Edge 8 (page 15) and Edge 10 again on the striped teatowel

Tea towel edges: from left to right, Two-colour teatowel II (page 20), Two-colour teatowel I (page 18) and Three-colour teatowel (page 19)

Kitchen handtowels: clockwise from back, Teatowel handtowel (page 20), Pineapple-topped kitchen towel (page 22), and Teatowel handtowel (page 20) in reverse colourway, and Shell half-towel handtowel (page 23) in two colourways

For the nursery: Clockwise from left: Bunny rug II (page 32), Dribble pillow (page 34), Bunny rug I (page 32) and Bunny rug III (page 33) in front

For the nursery: Singlet, socks and bib set (page 29) against the Cradle sheet (page 30) trimmed with a deep edge in soft yellow

FOR THE NURSERY

SINGLET, SOCKS AND BIB SET

Ideal for a quick easy hand-made gift for the newborn.

SINGLET

Materials
Baby s singlet with holes in elastic around neckline
5 g DMC Maeva No 10 crochet cotton
1.50 mm crochet hook
Small iron-on motif, or embroider your own design

1st round: Make 1dc in every hole evenly around the neck of the singlet, making sure not to have the work too tight, join with a sl st in first dc made.
2nd round: 1dc in same place as sl st, *3ch, 1tr in last dc, miss 2dc, 1dc in next dc, rep from * to end, join with a sl st in first dc made.
Fasten off.
Add decorative motif.

SOCKS

Materials
1 pair cotton socks

Small quantity DMC Maeva No 10 crochet cotton
1.50 mm crochet hook

Work both socks the same way.

1st round: With inside of sock facing, dc evenly around the top of the sock, keeping the number of dc divisible by 3, making sure you can still stretch the sock, join with a sl st in first dc made.

2nd round: 1ch, 1dc in same place as sl st, *3ch, 1tr in last dc, miss 2dc, 1dc in next dc, rep from * to end omitting the dc at end of last rep, join with a sl st in first dc. Fasten off.

BIB

Materials
Baby's bib
10 g DMC Maeva No 10 crochet cotton (this quantity will make edgings for about four bibs, depending on the size)
1.25 mm crochet hook, or hook that will go through the bib with ease
Iron-on or sew-on motif

Note: This pattern has only one row.

Work closer together around the curve of the bib.
With right side facing, insert hook into edge of bib, yoh and draw cotton through, make 2ch, 1dc in same place as join, *3ch, 1tr in last dc, miss the length of the stitch, 1dc in bib, 1dc in same place as last dc, rep from * all around the bib. Fasten off.
Iron or sew motif in right-hand corner.

CRADLE SHEET

This charming edge features little bears.

Materials
1 sheet 70 cm x 90 cm (27½" x 36")
20 g DMC Cébélia No 20 crochet cotton
1.25 mm crochet hook.
2 m (2¼ yds) of 3 mm (⅛") ribbon

Tension: 7 cm (2¾") for each pattern

Make 40ch.

1st row: 1tr in 6th ch from hook, *1ch, miss 1ch, 1tr in next ch, rep from * to end (there should be 18 spaces).

2nd row: 4ch, 1tr in next tr, *1ch, 1tr in next tr, rep from * to last 5ch, miss 1ch, 1tr in next ch.

3rd row: 4ch, 1tr in next tr, (1ch, 1tr in next tr) twice, (1tr in next 1ch sp, 1tr in next tr) twice, (1ch, 1tr in next tr) twice, (1tr in next 1ch sp, 1tr in next tr) twice, *1ch, 1tr in next tr, rep from * to last 4ch, miss 1ch, 1tr in next ch.

4th row: 4ch, 1tr in next tr, 1ch, 1tr in next tr, (1tr in next 1ch sp, 1tr in next tr) 3 times, (1ch, 1tr in next tr) 4 times, 1tr in each of next 4tr, 1tr in next 1ch sp, 1tr in next tr, 1ch, 1tr in each of next 5tr, 1tr in next 1ch sp, 1tr in next tr, 1ch, 1tr in next tr,1ch, miss 1ch, 1tr in next ch.

5th row: 4ch, 1tr in next tr, 1ch, 1tr in each of next 7tr, 1tr in next 1ch sp, 1tr in each of next 7tr, (1ch, 1tr in next tr) twice, (1tr in next 1ch sp, 1tr in next tr) twice, 1tr in each of next 6tr, 1ch, 1tr in next tr, 1ch, miss 1ch, 1tr in next ch.

6th row: 4ch, 1tr in next tr, 1ch, 1tr in each of next 11tr, 1tr in next 1ch sp, 1tr in next tr, 1ch, 1tr in each of next 15tr, 1ch, 1tr in next tr, 1ch, miss 1ch, 1tr in next ch.

7th row: 4ch, 1tr in next tr, 1ch, 1tr in next tr, 1ch, miss 1tr, 1tr in each of next 13tr, 1tr in next 1ch sp, 1tr in each of next 11tr, 1ch, miss 1tr, 1tr in next tr, 1ch, 1tr in next tr, 1ch, miss 1ch, 1tr in next ch.

8th row: 4ch, 1tr in next tr, 1ch, 1tr in next tr, 1ch, 1tr in each of next 25tr, (1ch, 1tr in next tr) twice, 1ch, miss 1ch, 1tr in next ch.

9th row: Same as 8th row.

10th row: 4ch, 1tr in next tr, 1ch, 1tr in next tr, 1tr in next 1ch sp, 1tr in each of next 11tr, 1ch, miss 1tr, 1tr in each of next 13tr, 1tr in next 1ch sp, 1tr in next tr, 1ch, 1tr in next tr, 1ch, miss 1ch, 1tr in next ch.

11th row: 4ch, 1tr in next tr, 1ch, 1tr in each of next 15tr, 1ch, 1tr in next tr, 1ch, miss 1tr, 1tr in each of next 11tr, 1ch, 1tr in next tr, 1ch, miss 1ch, 1tr in next ch.

12th row: 4ch, 1tr in next tr, 1ch, 1tr in each of next 7tr, (1ch, miss 1tr, 1tr in next tr) twice, 1ch, 1tr in next tr, 1ch, 1tr in each of next 7tr, 1ch, miss 1tr, 1tr in each of next 7tr, 1ch, 1tr in next tr, 1ch, miss 1ch, 1tr in next ch.

13th row: 4ch, 1tr in next tr, 1ch, 1tr in next tr, 1ch, miss 1tr, 1tr in each of next 5tr, 1ch, 1tr in next tr, 1ch, miss 1tr, 1tr in each of next 5tr, (1ch, 1tr in next tr) 4 times, (1ch, miss 1tr, 1tr in next tr) 3 times, 1ch, 1tr in next tr, 1ch, miss 1ch, 1tr in next ch.

14th row: 4ch, 1tr in next tr, (1ch, 1tr in next tr) 8 times, (1ch, miss 1tr, 1tr in next tr) twice, (1ch, 1tr in next tr) twice, (1ch, miss 1tr, 1tr in next tr) twice, (1ch, 1tr in next tr) twice, 1ch, miss 1ch, 1tr in next ch.

15th row: 4ch, *1tr in next tr, 1ch, rep from * to last 4ch, miss 1ch, 1tr in next ch.

16th row: Same as 15th row.

Rep 3rd to 16th rows for each pattern, omitting the 16th row at end of last rep, fasten off.

Sew crochet edge to top of sheet, thread ribbon through holes at top and bottom. Make three bows and sew to bottom of crochet work, one bow in the centre, and one bow each side evenly spaced from centre bow.

BUNNY RUG I

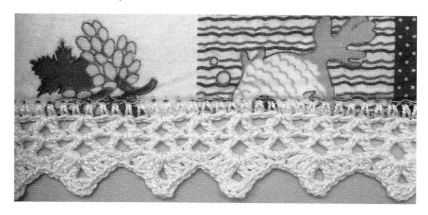

Materials

Fabric 90 cm (36") square, single or double thickness depending on warmth
required, with a hem no wider than 5 mm (³/₁₆"), or hemstitched edges
50 g DMC Maeva No 10 crochet cotton, or 50 g DMC Hermina 4-ply crochet cotton
1.75 mm and 2.00 mm crochet hooks

Note: If bunny rug has been hemstitched you may need to work 2dc in some
holes to get the required number of double crochet.

1st round: With right side facing, and 1.75 mm crochet hook, make dc evenly
divisible by 6 all around the bunny rug, working closer together around the
corners, join with a sl st in first dc made.
If using 4-ply cotton change to 2.00 mm crochet hook.
2nd round: 5ch, 1tr in same place as sl st, miss 2dc, *(1tr, 2ch, 1tr) in next dc,
rep from * to last 2dc, miss 2dc, join with a sl st in 3rd of 5ch made at beginning.
3rd round: sl st in first 2ch sp, 6ch, 1tr in same 2ch sp, *(1tr, 3ch, 1tr) in next 2ch
sp, rep from * to end, join with a sl st in 3rd of 6ch made at beginning.
4th round: sl st in first 3ch sp, (3ch, 2tr, 3ch, sl st in top of last tr, 3tr) in same
3ch sp, 1dc in next 3ch sp, *(3tr, 3ch, sl st in top of last tr, 3tr) in next 3ch sp, 1dc
in next 3ch sp, rep from * to end, join with a sl st in 3rd of 3ch made at beginning.
Fasten off.

BUNNY RUG II

Materials

Bunny rug approximately 90 cm (36") square
50 g DMC Hermina 4-ply cotton in main colour
20 g DMC Hermina 4-ply cotton in contrast colour
1.75 mm and 2.00 mm crochet hooks

Note: Work loops closer together around the corners on the first round.

1st round: With main colour and 1.75 mm crochet hook, right side facing, insert
hook into bunny rug edge, yoh and draw a loop through, make 1ch (this will be

the first dc), *4ch, miss the length of the 4ch, 1dc, rep from * to end omitting the dc at the end of last rep, join with a sl st in first dc made.
Change to 2.00 mm crochet hook.
2nd round: sl st into first 4ch loop, 6ch, 1tr in same loop, *(1tr, 3ch, 1tr) in next 4ch loop, rep from * to end, join with a sl st in 3rd of 6ch made at beginning.
3rd round: sl st in first 3ch sp, 6ch, 1tr in same sp, *(1tr, 3ch, 1tr) in next 3ch loop, rep from * to end, join with a sl st in 3rd of 6ch made at beginning. Fasten off main colour.
4th round: Join contrast cotton in any 3ch sp, *(2dc, 3ch, sl st in last dc made, 2dc) in next 3ch sp, rep from * to end, join with a sl st in first dc made. Fasten off.

BUNNY RUG III

Materials
Bunny rug 90 cm (36") square
40 g DMC Hermina 4-ply crochet cotton in main colour
40 g DMC Hermina 4-ply crochet cotton in contrast colour
1.75 mm and 2.00 mm crochet hooks

1st round: Right side facing, with main colour and 1.75 mm crochet hook, start in the corner, *make 6dc very close together, then make dc evenly divisible by 6 to the next corner, rep from * to end, join with a sl st in first dc made.
Change to 2.00 mm crochet hook.

2nd round: 1dc in same place as the sl st, *3ch, miss 2dc, (1tr, 3ch, 1tr) in next dc, 3ch, miss 2dc, 1dc in next dc, rep from * to end omitting the dc at end of last rep, join with a sl st in first dc made. Fasten off main colour.

3rd round: Join contrast colour in any 3ch loop, (3ch, 2tr, 3ch, 3tr) in same loop, 1ch, miss (3ch, 1dc, 3ch), *(3tr, 3ch, 3tr) in next 3ch sp, 1ch, miss (3ch, 1dc, 3ch), rep from * to end, join with a sl st in 3rd of 3ch made at beg. Fasten off.

DRIBBLE PILLOW

Materials
2 face washers 28 cm (11") square
50 g DMC Hermina 4-ply crochet cotton in main colour
30 g DMC Hermina 4-ply crochet cotton in contrast colour (these quantities will edge three pillows)
Polyester fibre filling
1.50 mm and 2.00 mm crochet hooks

Note: Work through both face washers together on three sides, and through one washer on the fourth side, leaving this side open for fibre filling.

1st round: Using main colour and 1.50 mm crochet hook or hook that will fit through both face washers with ease, insert hook through both face washers, into the edge over the hem, yoh and draw a loop through, make 1ch (this will be the first dc), work dc evenly divisible by 6 around three sides of pillow, then work last side through only one face washer, join with a sl st in first dc made. *Change to 2.00 mm crochet hook.*

2nd round: 1dc in same place as sl st, *miss 2dc, (1tr, 1ch, 1tr, 1ch, 1tr, 3ch, 1tr, 1ch, 1tr, 1ch, 1tr) in next dc, miss 2dc, 1dc in next dc, rep from * to end, omitting the dc at end of last rep, join with a sl st in first dc made. Fasten off main colour.

3rd round: Change to contrast colour, join cotton in first tr past dc, 1dc in same place as join, *1dc in next 1ch sp, 1dc in next tr, 1dc in next 1ch sp, 1dc in next tr, (1dc, 3ch, 1dc) in next 3ch sp, 1dc in next tr, 1dc in next 1ch sp, 1dc in next tr, 1dc in next 1ch sp, 1dc in next tr, miss 1dc, 1dc in next tr, rep from * to end, omitting 1dc at end of last rep, join with a sl st in first dc made. Fasten off.
Fill with polyester fibre filling, sew up opening.

FOR THE BATHROOM

HANDTOWEL I

Materials
1 handtowel
50 g DMC Hermina 4-ply crochet cotton (this quantity will make four edges)
2.00 mm crochet hook

1st row: 4ch, 1dtr in first ch, *4ch, 1dtr in top of last dtr, rep from * until length required, finishing with an odd number of 4ch loops, turn.
2nd row: 5ch, 1tr in first 4ch loop, 2ch, *1tr in next 4ch loop, 2ch, rep from * to end, 1tr in same place as first dtr in first row, turn.
3rd row: 3ch, *(1tr, 3ch, 1tr) in next tr, 1tr in next tr, rep from * working last tr in 3rd of 5ch, turn.
4th row: 3ch, *(2tr, 2ch, 2tr) in next 3ch sp, rep from * to end, working 1tr in 3rd of 3ch made at beg of last row, turn.
5th row: 3ch, *(2tr, 3ch, 1tr in top of last tr, 2tr) in next 2ch sp, rep from * to end, working 1tr in 3rd of 3ch made at beg of last row.
Fasten off.
Sew to edge of handtowel.

HANDTOWEL II

Materials
Handtowel
50 g DMC Hermina 4-ply cotton (this quantity will edge three average size handtowels)
2.00 mm crochet hook

Special abbreviation
(1dc, 2ch) at the beginning of a row will be called a tr throughout this pattern.

Make 12 ch.
1st row: 1tr in 4th ch from hook, 1tr in each ch to end (there should be 10tr counting the missed 3ch as 1tr), turn.
2nd row: (1dc, 2ch) in first tr, 1tr in each of next 2tr, 5ch, miss 4tr, 1tr in each of next 3tr, 4ch, sl st in base of tr just made, turn.
3rd row: 3ch, 2tr in 4ch sp, 3ch, 1dc in top of last tr made, 3tr in same 4ch space, 1tr in each of next 3tr, 5ch, 1tr in each of next 3tr, turn.
4th row: (1dc, 2ch) in first tr, 1tr in each of next 2tr, 4ch, 1dc over the two 5ch loops of two previous rows, 4ch, 1tr in each of next 3tr, 4ch, miss 1tr, sl st in next tr , turn.
5th row: Same as 3rd row.
6th row: (1dc, 2ch) in first tr, 1tr in each of next 2tr, 5ch, 1tr in each of next 3tr, 4ch, miss 1tr, sl st in next tr, turn.
7th row: 3ch, 2tr in 4ch sp, 3ch, 1dc in top of last tr made, 3tr in same 4ch sp, 1tr in each of next 3tr, 4ch, 1dc over the two 5ch loops of the two previous rows, 4ch, 1tr in each of next 3tr, turn.
8th row: Same as 6th row.
Rep 3rd to 8th rows to length required.
Next row: 3ch, 2tr in 4ch sp, 3ch, 1dc in top of last tr made, 3tr in same 4ch sp, 1tr in each of next 3tr, 4tr in 5ch loop, 1tr in each of next 3tr.
Fasten off.
Hand sew to edge of handtowel.

HANDTOWEL AND FACE WASHER SET 1

Materials
1 handtowel and 1 face washer
20 g DMC Cébélia No 10 crochet cotton, main colour
10 g DMC Cébélia No 10 crochet cotton, contrast colour
1.75 mm crochet hook, or hook that will fit through the handtowel or face washer
   with ease

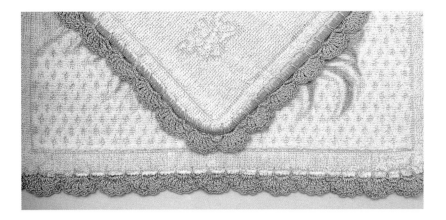

Notes:
✦ Handtowel and face washer are both worked the same.

✦ All hems should be no more than 1 cm (³/₈") wide; if wider, undo and hem again.

✦ There should be an even number of 5ch loops at the completion of 1st round, working closer together around the corners.

1st round: With main colour, right side facing, insert hook into edge, holding cotton at back of work, yoh and draw a loop through, make 1ch (this will be the first dc), *5ch, miss the length of the 5ch, 1dc, rep from * all around, omitting the dc at end of last rep, join with a sl st in first dc made.

2nd round: sl st in first 5ch loop, 4ch, 7dtr in same loop as sl st, 1dc in next 5ch loop, *8dtr in next 5ch loop, 1dc in next 5ch loop, rep from * to end, join with a sl st in 4th of 4ch made at beg. Fasten off main colour.

3rd round: Join contrast colour with a sl st between any dc and dtr, 1dc in same place, 3ch, *miss 2dtr, 1dc between dtr, 3ch, rep from * to next dc, 1dc in next space before dc, 1dc in space after dc, 3ch, rep from first * all around, ending with a dc in space before last dc, join with a sl st in first dc made.
Fasten off.

HANDTOWEL AND FACE WASHER SET II

Materials

1 face washer and handtowel
50 g DMC Hermina 4-ply crochet cotton (this quantity will make two sets)
1.75 mm and 2.00 mm crochet hooks

Notes

✦ All hems should be no more than 1 cm (³/₈") wide; if wider, undo and hem again.
✦ Work loops closer together around the corners in the first round.

Special abbreviation

cluster = yoh, insert hook where stated in pattern, yoh and draw a loop through, yoh, and take off 2 loops on hook, yoh, insert hook in same loop, yoh and draw a loop through, yoh and draw through 2 loops on the hook, yoh and draw through all 3 loops on hook.

FACE WASHER

1st round: Start anywhere, with right side facing and 1.75 mm crochet hook, or hook that will go through the washer with ease, work into the edge of the washer as follows: *1dc, 5ch, miss the length of the 5ch, rep from * evenly around the washer, join with a sl st in first dc made.
Change to 2.00 mm crochet hook.
2nd round: sl st into first 5ch loop, 3ch, 1tr in same loop, 3ch, 1tr in top of last tr made, cluster in same 5ch loop, *(cluster, 3ch, 1tr in top of cluster, cluster) in next 5ch loop, rep from * to end, join with a sl st in 3rd of 3ch made at beg.
Fasten off.

HANDTOWEL

Work top and bottom the same.
Use 1.75 mm crochet hook.
1st row: Make 1dc close to the corner, 5ch, miss the length of the 5ch, *1dc in edge, 5ch, miss the length of the 5ch, rep from * along the bottom or top of the handtowel, turn.
Change to 2.00 mm crochet hook.
2nd row: 3ch, *(cluster, 3ch, cluster) in 5ch loop, rep from * to end, 1tr in first dc, turn.
3rd row: 3ch, *(cluster, 3ch, 1tr in top of cluster, cluster) in next 3ch sp, rep from * to end, 1tr in 3rd of 3ch.
Fasten off.
Work other end the same, but don't fasten off.
Side border: Work along the sides as follows: 3ch, 1tr in top of last tr, 1dc in edge of crochet work, 3ch, 1tr in last dc, 1dc in first dc in 1st row, *3ch, 1tr in last dc, 1dc in edge of handtowel, rep from * along the side to end, working along the crochet work as before.
Fasten off.
Join cotton at other side of crochet work and work the same along second side.

GUEST TOWEL WITH PINEAPPLE EDGE

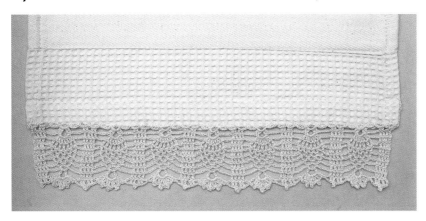

Materials

1 guest towel 30 cm (12") wide

20 g DMC Cébélia No 20 crochet cotton (this quantity will edge two towels)

1.25 mm crochet hook

1st row: 4ch, 1tr in 4th ch from hook, *4ch, 1tr in top of last tr, rep from * until required length, slightly stretched, finishing with a number of loops divisible by 5, plus 2.

2nd row: 3ch, 1tr in first 4ch loop, 2tr in next 4ch loop, *5ch, miss next 4ch loop, (2tr, 3ch, 2tr) in next 4ch loop, 5ch, miss next 4ch loop, (2tr in next 4ch loop) twice, rep from * to end.

3rd row: 1dc in first tr, 2ch, 1tr in each of next 3tr, *4ch, 7tr in next 3ch sp, 4ch, 1tr in each of next 4tr, rep from * working last tr in 3rd of 3ch.

4th row: 1dc in first tr, 2ch, 1tr in each of next 3tr, *3ch, 1tr in next tr, (1ch, 1tr in next tr) 6 times, 3ch, 1tr in each of next 4tr, rep from * working last tr in 2nd of 2ch.

5th row: 1dc in first tr, 2ch, 1tr in each of next 3tr, *(3ch, 1dc in next 1ch sp) 6 times, 3ch, 1tr in each of next 4tr, rep from * working last tr in 2nd of 2ch.

6th row: 1dc in first tr, 2ch, 1tr in each of next 3tr, *3ch, miss next 3ch sp, 1dc in next 3ch sp, (3ch, 1dc in next 3ch sp) 4 times, 3ch, 1tr in each of next 4tr, rep from * working last tr in 2nd of 2ch.

7th row: 1dc in first tr, 2ch, 1tr in each of next 3tr, *3ch, miss next 3ch sp,1dc in next 3ch sp, (3ch, 1dc in next 3ch sp) 3 times, 3ch, 1tr in each of next 4tr, rep from * working last tr in 2nd of 2ch.

8th row: 1dc in first tr, 2ch, 1tr in each of next 3tr, *4ch, miss next 3ch sp, 1dc in next 3ch sp, (3ch, 1dc in next 3ch sp) twice, 4ch, 1tr in each of next 4tr, rep from * working last tr in 2nd of 2ch.

9th row: 1dc in first tr, 2ch, 1tr in each of next 3tr, *6ch, 1dc in next 3ch sp, 3ch, 1dc in next 3ch sp, 6ch, 1tr in each of next 4tr, rep from * working last tr in 2nd of 2ch.

10th row: 1dc in first tr, 2ch, 1tr in each of next 3tr, *6ch, (1tr, 3ch, 1tr) in next 3ch sp, 6ch, 1tr in each of next 4tr, rep from * working last tr in 2nd of 2ch.

11th row: (Right side) 1dc in first tr, 2ch, 1tr in next tr, 3ch, 1dc in top of last tr, 1tr in each of next 2tr, *2ch, 1dc in next 6ch loop, 2ch, (2tr, 3ch, 1dc in top of last tr) 3 times in next 3ch sp, 2tr in same 3ch sp, 2ch, 1dc in next 6ch loop, 2ch, 1tr in each of next 2tr, 3ch, 1dc in top of last tr, 1tr in each of next 2tr, rep from * working last tr in 2nd of 2ch.

Fasten off.

Press lightly, sew to edge of guest towel.

BATH SET I

Materials

1 bath towel, handtowel and face washer
50 g DMC Hermina 4-ply crochet cotton
1.75 mm and 2.00 mm crochet hooks

FACE WASHER

Note: Work dc closer together around the corners.

1st round: With right side facing and 1.75 mm crochet hook, insert hook into edge, make 1ch (this will be the 1st dc), make dc all around the washer, finishing with a number divisible by 3, join with a sl st in first dc made.
Change to 2.00 mm crochet hook.
2nd round: 6ch, 1tr in same place as sl st, miss 2dc, *(1tr, 3ch, 1tr) in next dc, miss 2dc, rep from * to end, join with a sl st in 3rd of 6ch made at beg.
3rd round: sl st in first 3ch sp, (1dc, 1htr, 1tr, 1htr, 1dc) in same 3ch sp, *(1dc, 1htr, 1tr, 1htr, 1dc) in next 3ch sp, rep from * to end, join with a sl st in 3rd of 6ch made at beg.

HANDTOWEL

Use 2.00 mm crochet hook.
Make chain the length required, divisible by 4, plus 2.
1st row: 1tr in 4th ch from hook, 1tr in next ch, 2ch, miss 2ch, *1tr in each of next 2ch, 2ch, miss 2ch, rep from * to last, 3ch, 1tr in each ch to end, turn.
2nd row: 3ch, 1tr in each of next 2tr, 2ch, *1tr in each of the next 2tr, 2ch, rep from * to last 2tr and turning ch, 1tr in each of next 2tr, 1tr in 3rd of turning ch, turn.
3rd row: Same as 2nd row.
4th row: 3ch, 1tr in each of next 2tr, *1tr in next tr, 4ch, 1tr in next tr, rep from * to last 2tr and turning ch, 1tr in each of next 2tr, 1tr in 3rd of turning ch, turn.

5th row: 1dc in each of next 3tr, *(1dc, 1htr, 1tr, 1dtr, 1tr, 1htr, 1dc) in next 4ch, rep from * to last 2tr and turning ch, 1dc in each of next 2tr, 1dc in 3rd of turning ch, turn.
Fasten off.
Sew to handtowel.

BATH TOWEL

1st row: Same as 1st row of handtowel.
2nd, 3rd, 4th, 5th, and 6th rows: Same as 2nd row of handtowel.
7th row: Same as 4th row of handtowel.
8th row: Same as 5th row of handtowel.
Fasten off.
Sew to bath towel.

BATH SET II

Materials
1 bath towel (standard size), handtowel and face washer
50 g DMC Hermina 4-ply cotton
1.75 mm and 2.00 mm crochet hooks

Note: Work loops closer together around the corners in the first round.

FACE WASHER

1st round: Right side facing, use 1.75 mm crochet hook, or hook that will fit through the face washer with ease, insert hook into edge of face washer, 1ch (this will be the first dc), *4ch, miss the length of the 4ch, 1dc, rep from * all around the face washer, finishing with an even number of loops, omitting the dc at end of last rep, join with a sl st in first dc made.

Change to 2.00 mm crochet hook.

2nd round: sl st in first 4ch loop, 1ch, 1dc in same 4ch loop, *(1tr, 3ch, sl st in last tr, 1ch) 4 times in next 4ch loop, 1tr in same 4ch loop, 1dc in next 4ch loop, rep from * to end, omitting the dc at end of last rep, join with a sl st in first dc made.

Fasten off.

HANDTOWEL

Use 2.00 mm crochet hook.

1st row: 4ch, 1dtr in first ch, *4ch, 1dtr in top of last dtr, rep from * until length required, finishing with an even number of loops, turn.

2nd row: 3ch, *(1tr, 2ch, 1tr) in next 4ch loop, rep from * ending with 1tr in same place as first dtr in first row, turn.

3rd row: 3ch, *(1tr, 2ch, 1tr) in next 2ch sp, rep from * ending with 1tr in 3rd of 3ch made at beg of last row, turn.

4th row: 4ch, 1dc in next 2ch sp, *5ch, 1dc in next 2ch sp, rep from * to end, 4ch, 1dc in 3rd of 3ch made at beg of last row, turn.

5th row: sl st in first 4ch loop, 6ch, sl st in 3rd of 6ch, 1ch, 1tr in same 4ch loop, 3ch, sl st in last tr, 1ch, 1tr in same 4ch loop, 1dc in next 5ch loop, *(1tr, 3ch, sl st in last tr, 1ch) 4 times in next 5ch loop, 1tr in same 5ch loop, 1dc in next 5ch loop, rep from * to 4ch loop, (1tr in 4ch loop, 3ch, sl st in last tr, 1ch) twice in same 4ch loop, 1tr in same 4ch loop.

Fasten off.

Sew to handtowel.

BATH TOWEL

1st row: Same as 1st row of handtowel.

2nd row: Same as 2nd row of handtowel.

3rd, 4th, 5th, 6th and 7th rows: Same as 3rd row of handtowel.

8th row: Same as 4th row of handtowel.

9th row: Same as 5th row of handtowel.

Sew to bath towel.

FOR THE BEDROOM

HANDKERCHIEF I

Materials

1 handkerchief, not hemstitched
20 g DMC Cébélia No 40 crochet cotton (this quantity will edge four 25 cm [10"] square handkerchiefs)
0.75 mm crochet hook

Note: Work loops closer together around the corners.

1st round: With right side facing, insert hook into edge of handkerchief over hem, yoh and draw cotton through, 1ch (this will be the first dc), 5ch, miss the length of the 5ch, *1dc, 5ch, miss the length of the 5ch, rep from * to end, finishing with an even number of loops, join with a sl st in first dc made.
2nd round: sl st in first 5ch loop, 1dc in same loop, *7tr in next 5ch loop, 1dc in next 5ch loop, rep from * to end omitting the dc at end of last rep, join with a sl st in first dc.
3rd round: 1dc in same place as sl st, *1dc in next tr, 1htr in next tr, 1tr in next tr, (2dtr, 3ch, sl st in top of last dtr, 1dtr) in next tr, 1tr in next tr, 1htr in next tr, 1dc in next tr, 1dc in next dc, rep from * to end omitting the dc at end of last rep, join with a sl st in first dc made.

From the left: Handkerchiefs I and II

HANDKERCHIEF II

Materials

1 handkerchief, hemstitched

20 g DMC Cébélia No 40 crochet cotton (this quantity will edge three 25 cm [10"] square handkerchiefs)

0.75 mm crochet hook

Note: Work in multiples of 5. It may be necessary to work 2dc in some holes to end up with the required number of dc.

1st round: Start in corner hole, make 5dc in corner hole, *1dc in each hole to next corner, 5dc in corner hole, rep from * to end, omitting the 5dc at end of last rep, join with a sl st in first dc made.

2nd round: sl st in next 2dc, (4ch, 1tr, 2ch. 1tr, 1ch, 1tr) in same dc as last sl st, miss 4dc, *(1tr, 1ch, 1tr, 2ch, 1tr, 1ch, 1tr) in next dc, miss 4dc, rep from * to end, join with a sl st in 3rd of 4ch made at beg.

3rd round: sl st in each of next 2sts, sl st in 2ch sp, (3ch, 1tr, 3ch, 1dc in last tr, 3ch, 1dc in last dc, 3ch 1dc in last dc, 2tr) in same 2ch sp, *(2tr, 3ch, 1dc in last tr, 3ch, 1dc in last dc, 3ch, 1dc in last dc, 2tr) in next 2ch sp, rep from * to end, join with a sl st in 3rd of 3ch, fasten off.

PILLOWCASES

Dress up your pillowcases with this pretty edge.

Materials

Pair pillowcases

50 g DMC Maeva No 10 crochet cotton

1.75 mm crochet hook

60 cm (24") of 5 mm (³/₁₆") satin ribbon for each pillowcase

Bathroom handtowels: clockwise from left, Guest towel with pineapple edge (page 39), Handtowel I (page 35) and Handtowel II (page 35)

Handtowel and face washer sets: Set II (page 37) on the left, worked on blue, and Set I (page 36) worked in mauve on pretty florals

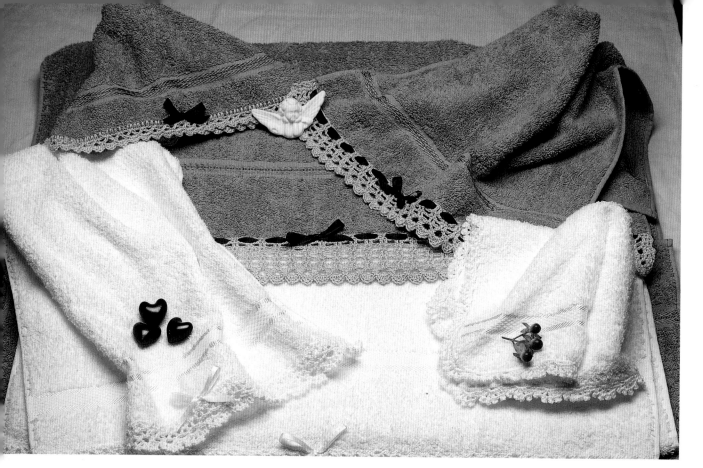

Bath sets: Bath set I (page 40) worked in white on white; Bath set II (page 41) worked in pale green on pale green, with a darker green ribbon insert

For the bedroom: Handkerchief I (page 43) on the left, Handkerchief II (page 44) on the right, in front of Pillowcases (page 44) trimmed in ecru

For the table: clockwise from left, Tray cloth I (page 52) and Tray cloth II (page 53) sitting on the Square tablecloth (page 54), with the Pineapple and heart edged doily (page 50) in the foreground

For the table: Place mats (page 59) sitting on the Round tablecloth (page 55)

*For the table:
clockwise from left,
Table cloth for one
(page 54), all in
white, and Table
cloth, serviettes
and serviette rings
(page 57) in blue
and white*

*Soft furnishings: Square cushion (page 61) with rose trim and Round cushion
(page 63), with the Curtain edging (page 60) in the foreground*

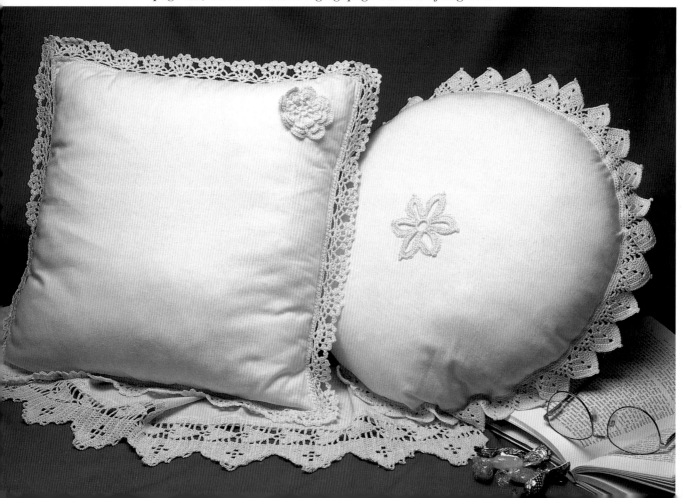

Tension: Width 6 rows = 6 cm (2¼"); length 6 rows = 4 cm (1½")

Make 11ch.

1st row: 1tr in 4th ch from hook, 2ch, miss 2ch, 1tr in next ch, 1ch, miss 1ch, 1tr in next ch, 1ch, miss 1ch, (1tr, 3ch, 1tr) in next ch, turn.

2nd row: 3ch (these will be referred to as turning ch throughout this pattern), 5tr in 3ch sp, 1tr in next tr, 1ch, 1tr in next tr, 1ch, 1tr in next tr, 2ch, 1tr in next tr, 1tr in turning ch, turn.

3rd row: 3ch, 1tr in next tr, 2ch, 1tr in next tr, 1ch, 1tr in next tr, 1ch, (1tr, 3ch, 1tr) in next tr, miss 2tr, (1tr, 3ch, 1tr) in next tr, miss 2tr, (1tr, 3ch, 1tr) in turning ch, turn.

4th row: 3ch, 5tr in first 3ch loop, 1dc in next 3ch loop, 5tr in next 3ch loop, 1tr in next tr, 1ch, 1tr in next tr, 1ch, 1tr in next tr, 2ch, 1tr in next tr, 1tr in turning ch, turn.

5th row: 3ch, 1tr in next tr, 2ch, 1tr in next tr, 1ch, 1tr in next tr, 1ch, (1tr, 3ch, 1tr) in next tr, miss 2tr, (1tr, 3ch, 1tr) in next tr, miss 2tr, (1tr, 3ch, 1tr) in next dc, miss 2tr, (1tr, 3ch, 1tr) in next tr, miss 2tr, (1tr, 3ch, 1tr) in turning ch, turn.

6th row: 3ch, 5tr in first 3ch loop, *1dc in next 3ch loop, 5tr in next 3ch loop, rep from * once, 1tr in next tr, 1ch, 1tr in next tr, 1ch, 1tr in next tr, 2ch, 1tr in next tr, 1tr in turning ch, turn.

7th row: 3ch, 1tr in next tr, 2ch, 1tr in next tr, 1ch, 1tr in next tr, 1ch (1tr, 3ch, 1tr) in next tr, turn.

Rep 2nd to 7th rows for the pattern, rep to required length, finishing on 6th row. Fasten off.

Thread ribbon through the 2ch spaces, sew edge to pillowcase.

FOR THE TABLE

DOILY WITH PINEAPPLE AND HEART EDGE

Materials
Circle of damask or linen 15 cm (6") in diameter, overlocked or with a hem 5 mm
   ($^3/_{16}$") wide
20 g DMC Cébélia No 30 crochet cotton
1.00 mm crochet hook, or hook to achieve an even tension

Tension: Eight 3ch loops to 4.5 cm (1¾")

1st round: Divide the material into four, place a marker in each quarter; starting
at one marker, insert hook into edge, yoh and draw yarn through, make 1ch (this
will be counted as the first dc), *3ch, miss the length of the 3ch, 1dc, rep from *
to next marker to give 20 3ch spaces, rep from first * to end, join with a sl st in
first dc made (there should be 80 3ch spaces).
2nd round: sl st in first 3ch sp, (3ch, 1tr, 2ch, 2tr) in same 3ch sp as the sl st, 3ch,
miss next 3ch sp, (2tr, 2ch, 2tr) in next 3ch sp, 3ch, miss two 3ch sps, 9dtr in next
3ch sp, *3ch, miss next two 3ch sps, (2tr, 2ch, 2tr) in next 3ch sp, 3ch, miss next
3ch sp, (2tr, 2ch, 2tr) in next 3ch sp, 3ch, miss next two 3ch sps, 9dtr in next 3ch
sp, rep from * to end, 3ch, join with a sl st in top of 3ch made at beg (10 patterns).
3rd round: sl st into next tr and 2ch sp, (3ch, 1tr, 2ch, 2tr) in same sp as last sl st,
2ch, (2tr, 2ch, 2tr) in next 2ch sp, 3ch, 1tr in next dtr, (1ch, 1tr in next dtr) 8
times, *3ch, (2tr, 2ch, 2tr) in next 2ch sp, 2ch, (2tr, 2ch, 2tr) in next 2ch sp, 3ch,
1tr in next dtr, (1ch, 1tr in next dtr) 8 times, rep from * to end, 3ch, join with a sl
st in top of 3ch made at beg.
4th round: sl st in next tr and 2ch sp, (3ch, 1tr, 2ch, 2tr) in same sp as last sl st,

1ch, miss next 2ch sp,(2tr, 2ch, 2tr) in next 2ch sp, 3ch, 1dc in next 1ch sp, (3ch, 1dc in next 1ch sp) 7 times, *3ch, (2tr, 2ch, 2tr) in next 2ch sp, 1ch, miss next 2ch sp, (2tr, 2ch, 2tr) in next 2ch sp, 3ch, 1dc in next 1ch sp, (3ch, 1dc in next 1ch sp) 7 times, rep from * to end, 3ch, join with a sl st in top of 3ch made at beg.

5th round: sl st in next tr and 2ch sp, (3ch, 1tr, 2ch, 2tr) in same sp as last sl st, 2ch, (2tr, 2ch, 2tr) in next 2ch sp, 3ch, miss next 3ch sp, 1dc in next 3ch sp, (3ch, 1dc in next 3ch sp) 6 times, *3ch, (2tr, 2ch, 2tr) in next 2ch sp, 2ch, (2tr, 2ch, 2tr) in next 2ch sp, 3ch, miss next 3ch sp, 1dc in next 3ch sp, (3ch, 1dc in next 3ch sp) 6 times, rep from * to end, 3ch, join with a sl st in top of 3ch made at beg.

6th round: sl st in next tr and 2ch sp, (3ch, 1tr, 2ch, 2tr) in same sp as last sl st, 2ch, 1dc in next 2ch sp, 2ch, (2tr, 2ch, 2tr) in next 2ch sp, 3ch, miss next 3ch sp, 1dc in next 3ch sp, (3ch, 1dc in next 3ch sp) 5 times, *3ch, (2tr, 2ch, 2tr) in next 2ch sp, 2ch, 1dc in next 2ch sp, 2ch, (2tr, 2ch, 2tr) in next 2ch sp, 3ch, miss next 3ch sp, 1dc in next 3ch sp, (3ch, 1dc in next 3ch sp) 5 times, rep from * to end, 3ch join with a sl st in top of 3ch made at beg.

7th round: sl st in next tr and 2ch sp, (3ch, 1tr, 2ch, 2tr) in same sp as last sl st, 2ch, 1dc in next 2ch sp, 3ch, 1dc in next 2ch sp, 2ch, (2tr, 2ch, 2tr) in next 2ch sp, 3ch, miss next 3ch sp, 1dc in next 3ch sp, (3ch, 1dc in next 3ch sp) 4 times, *3ch, (2tr, 2ch, 2tr) in next 2ch sp, 2ch, 1dc in next 2ch sp, 3ch, 1dc in next 2ch sp, 2ch, (2tr, 2ch, 2tr) in next 2ch sp, 3ch, miss next 3ch sp, 1dc in next 3ch sp, (3ch, 1dc in next 3ch sp) 4 times, rep from * to end, 3ch, join with a sl st in top of 3ch made at beg.

8th round: sl st in next tr and 2ch sp, (3ch, 1tr, 2ch, 2tr) in same sp as last sl st, 2ch, 7tr in next 3ch sp, 2ch, miss next 2ch sp, (2tr, 2ch, 2tr) in next 2ch sp, 3ch, miss next 3ch sp, 1dc in next 3ch sp, (3ch, 1dc in next 3ch sp) 3 times, *3ch, (2tr, 2ch, 2tr) in next 2ch sp, 2ch, 7tr in next 3ch sp, 2ch, miss next 2ch sp, (2tr, 2ch, 2tr) in next 2ch sp, 3ch, miss next 3ch sp, 1dc in next 3ch sp, (3ch, 1dc in next 3ch sp) 3 times, rep from * to end, 3ch, join with a sl st in top of 3ch made at beg.

9th round: sl st in next tr and 2ch sp, (3ch, 1tr, 2ch, 2tr) in same sp as last sl st, 2ch, 2tr in next tr, 1tr in each of next 5tr, 2tr in next tr, 2ch, miss next 2ch sp, (2tr, 2ch, 2tr) in next 2ch sp, 3ch, miss next 3ch sp, 1dc in next 3ch sp, (3ch, 1dc in next 3ch sp) twice, *3ch, (2tr, 2ch, 2tr) in next 2ch sp, 2ch, 2tr in next tr, 1tr in each of the next 5tr, 2tr in next tr, 2ch, miss next 2ch sp, (2tr, 2ch, 2tr) in next 2ch sp, 3ch, miss next 3ch sp, 1dc in next 3ch sp, (3ch, 1dc in next 3ch sp) twice, rep from * to end, 3ch, join with a sl st in top of 3ch made at beg.

10th round: sl st in next tr and 2ch sp, (3ch, 1tr, 2ch, 2tr) in same sp as last sl st, 3ch, 2tr in next tr, 1tr in next tr, 2tr in next tr, 3ch, miss 3tr, 2tr in next tr, 1tr in next tr, 2tr in next tr, 3ch, (2tr, 2ch, 2tr) in next 2ch sp, 3ch, miss next 3ch sp, 1dc in next 3ch sp, 3ch, 1dc in next 3ch sp, *3ch, (2tr, 2ch, 2tr) in next 2ch sp, 3ch, 2tr in next tr, 1tr in next tr, 2tr in next tr, 3ch, miss 3tr, 2tr in next tr, 1tr in next tr, 2tr in next tr, 3ch, (2tr, 2ch, 2tr) in next 2ch sp, 3ch, miss next 3ch sp, 1dc in next 3ch sp, 3ch, 1dc in next 3ch sp, rep from * to end, 3ch, join with a sl st in top of 3ch made at beg.

11th round: sl st in next tr and 2ch sp, (3ch, 1tr , 2ch, 2tr) in same sp as last sl st, 3ch, miss next 3ch sp, 2tr in next tr, 1tr in next tr, 2tr in next tr, 3ch, 1dc in next 3ch sp, 3ch, miss 2tr, 2tr in next tr, 1tr in next tr, 2tr in next tr, 3ch, (2tr, 2ch, 2tr) in next 2ch sp, 4ch, miss next 3ch sp, 1dc in next 3ch sp, *4ch, (2tr, 2ch, 2tr) in next 2ch sp, 3ch, miss next 3ch sp, 2tr in next tr, 1tr in next tr, 2tr in next tr, 3ch, 1dc in next 3ch sp, 3ch, miss 2tr, 2tr in next tr, 1tr in next tr, 2tr in next tr, 3ch, (2tr, 2ch, 2tr) in next 2ch sp, 4ch, miss next 3ch sp, 1dc in next 3ch sp, rep from * to end, 4ch, join with a sl st in top of 3ch made at beg.

12th round: sl st in next tr and 2ch sp, (3ch, 1tr, 3ch, 1tr in top of last tr, 2tr) in same sp as last sl st, *3ch, 1tr in top of last tr, miss 3ch, 1tr in each of next 2tr, 3ch, 1tr in top of last tr, miss 1tr, 1tr in each of next 2tr, 3ch, 1tr in top of last tr, 2tr in next dc, 3ch, 1tr in top of last tr, 1tr in each of next 2tr, 3ch, 1tr in top of last tr, miss 1tr, 1tr in each of next 2tr, 3ch, 1tr in top of last tr, (2tr, 3ch, 1tr in top of last tr, 2tr) in next 2ch sp, 3ch, 1tr in top of last tr, (2tr, 3ch, 1tr in top of last tr, 2tr) in next 2ch sp, rep from * to end, omitting from (2tr, 3ch, 1tr in top of last tr, 2tr) in next 2ch sp at end of last rep, join with a sl st in top of 3ch made at beg. Fasten off.

TRAY CLOTH I

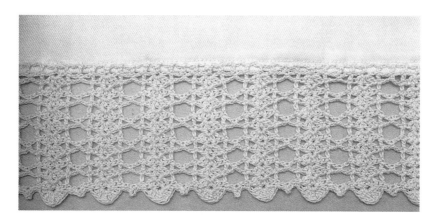

Materials

30 cm x 38 cm (12" x 15") fabric with 1 cm (³/₈") hem all around, measuring 27 cm x 35 cm (10½" x 13¾") when hemmed

20 g DMC Cébélia No 20 crochet cotton

1.25 mm crochet hook

Tension: 2 patterns = 5 cm (2")

Note: If making a wider cloth add 12 ch for each pattern repeat required.

Make 131ch.

1st row: 1tr in 4th ch from hook, *2ch, miss 2ch, 1tr in next ch, rep from * to last ch, 1tr in last ch.

2nd row: 1dc in first tr, 2ch, 1tr in next tr, 2ch, 1dc in next tr, 2ch, 1tr in next tr, *5tr in next tr, 1tr in next tr, 2ch, 1dc in next tr, 2ch, 1tr in next tr, rep from * to end, 1tr in 3rd of 3ch missed at the beginning of first row.

3rd row: 1dc in first tr, 2ch, 1tr in next tr, 5ch, 1tr in next tr, *miss 2tr, 5tr in next tr, miss 2tr, 1tr in next tr, 5ch, 1tr in next tr, rep from * to end, 1tr in 2nd of 2ch.

4th row: 1dc in first tr, 2ch, 1tr in next tr, 2ch, miss 2ch, 1dc in next ch, 2ch, 1tr in next tr, miss 2tr, *5tr in next tr, miss 2tr, 1tr in next tr, 2ch, miss 2ch, 1dc in next ch, 2ch, 1tr in next tr, rep from * to end, 1tr in 2nd of 2ch.

Rep 3rd and 4th rows three times, then 3rd row once.

12th row: (Right side), 1dc in first tr, 2ch, 1tr in next tr, 1ch, miss 2ch, (1dc, 3ch,

1dc) in next ch, 1ch, *1dc in next tr, miss 2tr, (3tr, 1dtr, 3tr) in next tr, miss 2tr, 1dc in next tr, 1ch, miss 2ch, (1dc, 3ch, 1dc) in next ch, 1ch, rep from * working 1tr in last tr, and 1tr in 2nd of 2ch.
Fasten off.
Make second piece.
Sew to each end of cloth.

TRAY CLOTH II

Materials
Linen or other fabric of your choice, measuring 24 cm x 38 cm (9½" x 15") when hemmed with a 5 mm (³/₁₆") hem
20 g DMC Cébélia No 20 crochet cotton
1.25 mm crochet hook

1st round: Starting before a corner, insert hook into work over hem, yoh and draw cotton through, make 1ch (this will be the first dc), make 2dc, 4ch, 3dc in centre of corner, 4ch, 3dc in other side of corner, 4ch, *3dc, 4ch, miss the length of the 4ch, rep from * to next corner, (3dc, 4ch, 3dc, 4ch, 3dc) as first corner, 4ch, rep from first * to end, omitting the corner at end of last rep, join with a sl st in first dc.
2nd round: sl st in next dc, 1dc in same dc as sl st, 2ch, *(2tr, 3ch, 2tr) in next 4ch loop, 2ch, miss next dc, 1dc in next dc, 2ch, rep from * omitting dc at end of last rep, join with a sl st in first dc.
3rd round: sl st in first 2ch sp, 3ch, 7tr in next 3ch sp, *holding last loop of each tr on hook make 1tr in each of next two 2ch sps, yoh and draw through all 3 loops on hook, 7tr in next 3ch sp, rep from * to last 2ch sp, 1tr in 2ch sp, join with a sl st in 3rd of 3ch made at beg.
4th round: sl st in first tr, 3ch, holding loop of each tr on hook make 1tr in each of the next 2tr, yoh and draw through all three loops on hook, *5ch, (holding last loop of each tr on hook make 1tr in same place as last tr, 1tr in each of the next 2tr), yoh and draw through all 4 loops on hook, rep from * once, miss 2tr worked together, holding last loop of each tr on hook make 1tr in each of the next 3tr, yoh and draw through all 4 loops on hook, rep from first * omitting the last 3tr at end of last rep, join with a sl st in top of first group of stitches made at beg.
Fasten off.

TABLECLOTH FOR ONE

Materials

Fabric with finished size of 48 cm x 72 cm (19" x 28½"), with hem no more than 1 cm (³⁄₈") wide, or linen teatowel
50 g DMC Hermina 4-ply crochet cotton
1.75 mm crochet hook

Note: Work loops closer together around the corners.

1st round: Insert hook into cloth over the hem, yoh and draw yarn through, make 1ch (this will be the first dc), 1dc in same place as the first dc, *4ch, miss the length of the 4ch, 2dc in same place, rep from * to end, 4ch, join with a sl st in first dc made.

2nd round: sl st in next dc, sl st in first 4ch loop, (3ch, 1tr, 2ch, 2tr) in same 4ch loop as the sl st, *(2tr, 2ch, 2tr) in next 4ch loop, rep from * to end, join with a sl st in top of 3ch made at beg.

3rd round: sl st in next tr and 2ch sp, 7ch, 1tr in same sp as sl st, *(1tr, 4ch, 1tr) in next 2ch sp, rep from * to end, join with a sl st in 3rd of 7ch made at beg.

4th round: sl st in first 4ch loop, (3ch, 1tr, 3ch, 1dc in last tr made, 2tr) in same 4ch loop as the sl st, *(2tr, 3ch, 1dc in last tr made, 2tr) in next 4ch loop, rep from * to end, join with a sl st in top of 3ch made at beg.
Fasten off.

SQUARE TABLECLOTH

Materials
135 cm (53") square tablecloth
75 g DMC Maeva No 10 crochet cotton
1.50 mm crochet hook

1st round: Starting 5 mm (³/₁₆") before a corner, insert hook over hem and into the tablecloth, yoh and draw a loop through, make 1ch (this will be the first dc), 1dc in same place as last dc, 4ch, miss 5 mm (³/₁₆") past the corner, 2dc in same place, 4ch, *miss the length of the 4ch, 2dc in same place, 4ch, rep from * to 5 mm (³/₁₆") before next corner, 2dc in same place, 4ch, miss 5 mm (³/₁₆") past the corner, 2dc in same place, 4ch, rep from first * to end, omitting the last corner at end of last rep, join with a sl st in first dc made.

2nd round: sl st in next dc, sl st in first 4ch loop, (3ch, 1tr, 3ch, 2tr, 3ch, 2tr) in same 4ch loop as sl st, *(1tr, 4ch, 1tr) in next 4ch loop, rep from * to next corner space, (2tr, 3ch, 2tr, 3ch 2tr) in corner sp, rep from first * to end omitting the corner at end of last rep, join with a sl st in 3rd of 3ch made at beg.

3rd round: sl st in next tr, sl st in first 3ch sp, (3ch, 1tr, 3ch, 2tr) in same 3ch sp as sl st, 3ch, (2tr, 3ch, 2tr) in next 3ch sp, *(1tr, 4ch, 1tr) in next 4ch loop, rep from * to next corner, (2tr, 3ch, 2tr) in next 3ch sp, 3ch, (2tr, 3ch, 2tr) in next 3ch sp, rep from first * to end, omitting the corner at end of last rep, join with a sl st in 3rd of 3ch made at beg.

4th round: sl st in next tr, sl st in 3ch sp, 3ch, 4tr in same 3ch sp, 5tr in each of the next two 3ch spaces, *5tr in next 4ch loop, rep from * to next corner, 5tr in each of the next three 3ch spaces, rep from first * to end omitting the corner at end of last rep, join with a sl st in 3rd of 3ch made at beg.

5th round: 1dc in same place as sl st, 7ch, sl st in 4th ch from hook, 3ch, miss 3tr, 1dc in next tr, 1dc in next tr, *7ch, sl st in 4th ch from hook, 3ch, miss 3tr, 1dc in next tr, 1dc in next tr, rep from * to end omitting dc at end of last rep, join with a sl st in first dc made.
Fasten off.

ROUND TABLECLOTH

Materials
Round tablecloth 180 cm (70") diameter
150 g DMC Maeva No 10 crochet cotton, main colour

30 g DMC Cébélia No 10 crochet cotton, contrast colour
1.75 mm crochet hook

Tension: 4 x 3ch loops to 4 cm (1½")

1st round: With main colour, insert hook into edge of tablecloth, yoh and draw yarn through, make 1ch (this will be counted as the first dc), *3ch, miss the length of the 3ch, 1dc, rep from * to end, having four 3ch loops for every pattern repeat, omitting the dc at end of last rep, join with a sl st in first dc made at beg.

2nd round: sl st into first 3ch sp, 6ch, 1tr in same space as sl st, 5ch, miss next 3ch sp, 1dc in next 3ch sp, 5ch, miss next 3ch sp, *(1tr, 3ch, 1tr) in next 3ch sp, 5ch, miss next 3ch sp, 1dc in next 3ch sp, 5ch, miss next 3ch sp, rep from * to end, join with a sl st in 3rd of 6ch made at the beg.

3rd round: sl st in first 3ch sp, (3ch, 1tr, 3ch, 2tr) in same sp as sl st, 3ch, 1dc in next 5ch loop, 3ch, 1dc in next 5ch loop, 3ch, *(2tr, 3ch, 2tr) in next 3ch sp, 3ch, 1dc in next 5ch loop, 3ch, 1dc in next 5ch loop, 3ch, rep from * to end, join with a sl st in top of 3ch made at beg.

4th round: sl st in next tr, 3ch, (2tr, 3ch, 2tr) in next 3ch sp, 1tr in next tr, 4ch, miss next 3ch sp, 1dc in next 3ch sp, 4ch, * miss next tr, 1tr in next tr, (2tr, 3ch, 2tr) in next 3ch sp, 1tr in next tr, 4ch, miss next 3ch sp, 1dc in next 3ch sp, 4ch, rep from * to end, join with a sl st in top of 3ch made at beg.

5th round: sl st in next tr, 3ch, 1tr in next tr, (2tr, 3ch, 2tr) in next 3ch sp, 1tr in each of next 2tr, 2ch, 1dc in next 4ch loop, 3ch, 1dc in next 4ch loop, 2ch, *miss 1tr, 1tr in each of next 2tr, (2tr, 3ch, 2tr) in next 3ch sp, 1tr in each of next 2tr, 2ch, 1dc in next 4ch loop, 3ch, 1dc in next 4ch loop, 2ch, rep from * to end, join with a sl st in top of 3ch made at beg.

6th round: sl st in next tr, 3ch, 1tr in each of next 2tr, (2tr, 3ch, 2tr) in next 3ch sp, 1tr in each of next 3tr, 3ch, 1dc in next 3ch sp, 3ch, *miss 1tr, 1tr in each of next 3tr, (2tr, 3ch, 2tr) in next 3ch sp, 1tr in each of next 3tr, 3ch, 1dc in next 3ch sp, 3ch, rep from * to end, join with a sl st in top of 3ch made at beg.

7th round: sl st in next tr, 3ch, 1tr in each of next 3tr, (2tr, 3ch, 2tr) in next 3ch sp, 1tr in each of next 4tr, 1ch, 1dc in next 3ch sp, 3ch, 1dc in next 3ch sp, 1ch, *miss 1tr, 1tr in each of next 4tr, (2tr, 3ch, 2tr) in next 3ch sp, 1tr in each of next 4tr, 1ch, 1dc in next 3ch sp, 3ch, 1dc in next 3ch sp, 1ch, rep from * to end, join with a sl st in top of 3ch made at beg.

8th round: sl st in next tr, 3ch, 1tr in each of next 4tr, (2tr, 3ch, 2tr) in next 3ch sp, 1tr in each of next 5tr, 2ch, 1dc in next 3ch sp, 2ch, *miss 1tr, 1tr in each of next 5tr, (2tr, 3ch, 2tr) in next 3ch sp, 1tr in each of next 5tr, 2ch, 1dc in next 3ch sp, 2ch, rep from * to end, join with a sl st in top of 3ch made at beg, fasten off main colour.

9th round: Join contrast with a sl st in same place as sl st, 1dc in same place, 1dc in each of next 6tr, *(1dc, 5ch, 1dc, 7ch, 1dc, 5ch, 1dc) in next 3ch sp, 1dc in each of next 7tr, 1dc in next 2ch sp, 1dc in next 2ch sp, 1dc in each of next 7tr, rep from * to end omitting the 7dc at end of last rep, join with a sl st in first dc made, fasten off.

TABLECLOTH, SERVIETTES AND SERVIETTE RINGS

Materials

132 cm (52") square tablecloth, with hem no more than 1 cm ($^3/_8$") wide
4 serviettes each 43 cm (17") square, with hems no more than 1 cm ($^3/_8$") wide
100 g DMC Maeva No 10 crochet cotton, main colour
30 g DMC Cébélia No 10 crochet cotton, contrast colour
1.75 mm crochet hook

Alternative

Rectangular tablecloth 132 cm x 178 cm (52" x 70"), with hem no more than 1 cm
   ($^3/_8$") wide
6 serviettes 43 cm (17") square, with hems no more than 1 cm ($^3/_8$") wide
200 g DMC Maeva No 10 crochet cotton, main colour
60 g DMC Cébélia No 10 crochet cotton, contrast colour
1.75 mm crochet hook

Note: There should be an even number of 5ch loops at the completion of 1st round, working closer together around the corners.

TABLECLOTH

1st round: With main colour, right side facing, insert hook into edge, holding cotton at the back of work, yoh and draw a loop through, make 1ch (this will be the first dc), *5ch, miss the length of the 5ch (about 1.5 cm), 1dc, rep from * all around, omitting the dc at end of last rep, join with a sl st in first dc made.

2nd round: sl st in first 5ch loop, 1dc in same loop, 3ch, *(3tr, 3ch, 3tr) in next 5ch loop, 3ch, 1dc in next 5ch loop, 3ch, rep from * to end, join with a sl st in first dc.

3rd round: 1dc in same place as sl st, 3ch, *miss 3ch, (3tr, 3ch, 3tr) in next 3ch loop, 3ch, 1dc in next dc, 3 ch, rep from * to end, omitting 1dc and 3ch at end of last rep, join with a sl st in first dc made.

4th round: 1ch, 1dc in same place as sl st, *3ch, miss 3ch, (1tr, 1ch) 5 times in next 3ch loop, 1tr in same loop, 3ch, 1dc in next dc, rep from * to end, omitting the dc at end of last rep, join with a sl st in first dc, fasten off main colour.

5th round: Join contrast in same place as sl st, 1dc in same place as join, *(3ch, 1dc in next 1ch sp) 5 times, 3ch, 1dc in next dc, rep from * to end, omitting the dc at end of last rep, join with a sl st in first dc made.
Fasten off.

SERVIETTES

1st round: Same as 1st round of tablecloth.
2nd round: Same as 2nd round of tablecloth.
3rd round: Same as 4th round of tablecloth.
4th round: Same as 5th round of tablecloth.

SERVIETTE RINGS

Materials
10 g DMC Cébélia No 10 crochet cotton
1.75 mm crochet hook
4 curtain rings 3 cm (1¼") diameter (or size preferred)

1st round: Join cotton over curtain ring and work in dc until the ring is completely covered, join with a sl st in first dc made.
2nd round: *5ch, miss 4dc, 1dc in next dc, rep from * 6 times, turn.
3rd round: 3ch, leaving last loop of each tr on hook, make 2tr in first 5ch loop, yoh and draw through all 3 loops on hook, 3ch, *leaving last loop of each on hook make 3tr in same loop, yoh and draw through all 4 loops on hook, 3ch, rep from * once, 1dc in next 5ch loop, 3ch, **leaving last loop of each on hook make 3tr in next 5ch loop, yoh and draw through all 4 loops on hook, 3ch, rep from ** twice in same loop, 1dc in next 5ch loop, 3ch, rep from first ** twice, omitting the 1dc and 3ch at end of last rep.
Fasten off.

PLACE MATS

Materials

Oval place mats to measure 28 cm x 40 cm (11" x 16") when hemstitched
15 g DMC Cébélia No 10 crochet cotton for each place mat
1.50 mm crochet hook

1st round: Insert hook into any hole, yoh and draw cotton through, make 1ch (this will be the first dc), make 1dc in each hole, keeping the number of dc divisible by 8 (you may have to work 2dc in some holes to get the required number), join with a sl st in first dc.

2nd round: 3ch, 2tr in same dc as sl st, 2ch, miss 3dc, (1tr, 2ch, 1tr) in next dc, 2ch, miss 3dc, *3tr in next dc, 2ch, miss 3dc, (1tr, 2ch, 1tr) in next dc, 2ch, miss 3dc, rep from * to end, join with a sl st in 3rd of 3ch.

3rd round: 3ch, 1tr in same place as sl st, 1tr in next tr, 2tr in next tr, 3ch, miss next 2ch sp, 1dc in next 2ch sp, 3ch, *2tr in next tr, 1tr in next tr, 2tr in next tr, 3ch, miss next 2ch sp, 1dc in next 2ch sp, 3ch, join with a sl st in 3rd of 3ch.

4th round: 5ch, *1tr in next tr, 2ch, rep from * to end, join with a sl st in 3rd of 5ch made at beg.

5th round: sl st in first 2ch sp, (1dc, 3ch, 1dc) in same 2ch sp as sl st, (1dc, 3ch, 1dc in next 2ch sp) 3 times, 1dc in next 2ch sp, *(1dc, 3ch, 1dc in next 2ch sp) 4 times, 1dc in next 2ch sp, rep from * to end, join with a sl st in first dc.
Fasten off.

SOFT FURNISHINGS

CURTAINS

Materials

Curtains length and width required

100 g DMC Maeva No 10 crochet cotton — this quantity will make approximately 170 cm (67")

1.75 mm crochet hook

Tension: 10 cm (4") in width at 7th row.

Make 25ch.

1st row: 1tr in 4th ch from hook, 1tr in each of next 3ch, 5ch, miss 3ch, 1dc in next ch, 5ch, miss 3ch, 1dc in next ch, 5ch, miss 3ch, 1tr in each of the next 7ch, turn.

2nd row: 9ch, 1tr in 8th and 9th ch from hook, 1tr in each of the next 7tr, 5ch, miss next 5ch loop, 3tr in next 5ch loop, 5ch, 1tr in each of the next 5tr, turn.

3rd row: (1dc, 2ch) in first tr, 1tr in each of next 4tr, 4ch, 2tr in next tr, 1tr in next tr, 2tr in next tr, 4ch, 1tr in each of next 9tr, 1tr in each of next 2ch, turn.

4th row: 9ch, 1tr in 8th and 9th ch from hook, 1tr in each of the next 11tr, 3ch, 2tr in next tr, 1tr in each of next 3 tr, 2tr in next tr, 3ch, 1tr in each of next 5tr, turn.

5th row: (1dc, 2ch) in first tr, 1tr in each of next 4tr, 2ch, 2tr in next tr, 1tr in each of next 5tr, 2tr in next tr, 2ch, 1tr in each of next 13tr, 1tr in each of next 2ch, turn.

6th row: 9ch, 1tr in 8th and 9th ch from hook, 1tr in each of next 6tr, 2ch, miss 2tr, 1tr in each of next 7tr, 1ch, 2tr in next tr, 1tr in each of next 2tr, 3ch, miss 1tr, 1dc in next tr, 3ch, miss 1tr, 1tr in each of next 2tr, 2tr in next tr, 1ch, 1tr in each of next 5tr, turn.

7th row: (1dc, 2ch) in first tr, 1tr in each of next 4tr, 5ch, 1dc in next 3ch sp, 5ch, 1dc in next 5ch sp, 5ch, miss 4tr, 1tr in each of next 4tr, 2ch, miss 2tr, 1tr in next tr, 2ch, miss 2tr, 1tr in next tr, 2ch, miss 2tr, 1tr in each of next 5tr, 2ch, miss 2ch, 1tr in next ch, turn.

8th row: 5ch, 1tr in each of next 5tr, 2tr in 2ch sp, 1tr in next tr, 2ch, 1tr in next tr, 2tr in next 2ch sp, 1tr in each of next 4tr, 5ch, miss next 5ch loop, 3tr in next 5ch loop, 5ch, 1tr in each of next 5tr, turn.

9th row: (1dc, 2ch) in first tr, 1tr in each of next 4tr, 4ch, 2tr in next tr, 1tr in next tr, 2tr in next tr, 4ch, 1tr in each of next 7tr, 2tr in 2ch sp, 1tr in each of next 6tr, turn.

10th row: 5ch, miss 2tr, 1tr in each of next 13tr, 3ch, 2tr in next tr, 1tr in each of next 3tr, 2tr in next tr, 3ch, 1tr in each of next 5tr, turn.

11th row: (1dc, 2ch) in first tr, 1tr in each of next 4tr, 2ch, 2tr in next tr, 1tr in each of next 5tr, 2tr in next tr, 2ch, 1tr in each of next 11tr, turn.

12th row: 5ch, miss 2tr, 1tr in each of next 9tr, 1ch, 2tr in next tr, 1tr in each of next 2tr, 3ch, miss 1tr, 1dc in next tr, 3ch, miss 1tr, 1tr in each of next 2tr, 2tr in next tr, 1ch, 1tr in each of next 5tr.

13th row: (1dc, 2ch) in first tr, 1tr in each of next 4tr, 5ch, 1dc in next 3ch sp, 5ch, 1dc in next 3ch sp, 5ch, miss 4tr, 1tr in each of next 7tr, turn.

Rep rows 2 to 13 until work measures length required, omitting the 7ch at end of last rep.

Fasten off.

Sew to bottom of curtains.

SQUARE CUSHION

Materials
Two pieces fabric 40 cm (16") square
No 16 cushion insert
20 g DMC Maeva No 10 crochet cotton
1.50 mm crochet hook

With two pieces of fabric right sides together, hemstitch three sides through both thicknesses. On the fourth side hemstitch only through one thickness, leaving an opening for the cushion insert.

Note: This pattern uses 10dc to the pattern; you may need to work 2dc in some holes to get the number of dc needed on each side.

1st round: Starting one hole before corner, 2dc in same sp, *6dc in corner hole, 2dc in next hole, 1dc in each hole until one hole before the next corner, 2dc in next hole, rep from * to end omitting the 2dc at end of last rep, join with a sl st in first dc (the number of dc should be divisible by 10).

2nd round: 1dc in same place as sl st, 5ch, *miss 4dc, (1tr, 3ch, 1tr) in next dc, 5ch, miss 4dc, 1dc in next dc, 5ch, rep from * to last 9dc, miss 4dc, (1tr, 3ch, 1tr) in next dc, join with 2ch, miss 4dc, 1tr in first dc (this brings the work into position to start the next round).

3rd round: 1ch, 1dc over the last tr, 3ch, 1dc in next 5ch loop, 2ch, (1tr, 1ch, 1tr, 1ch, 1tr, 1ch, 1tr, 1ch, 1tr, 1ch, 1tr, 1ch, 1tr) in corner sp, 2ch, 1dc in next 5ch loop, 3ch, 1dc in next 5ch loop, 2ch, *(1tr, 1ch, 1tr, 1ch, 1tr, 1ch, 1tr, 1ch, 1tr) in next 3ch sp, 2ch, 1dc in next 5ch loop, 3ch, 1dc in next 5ch loop, 2ch, rep from * to next corner, (1tr, 1ch, 1tr, 1ch, 1tr, 1ch, 1tr, 1ch, 1tr, 1ch, 1tr, 1ch, 1tr) in next 3ch sp, 2ch, 1dc in next 5ch loop, 3ch, 1dc in next 5ch loop, 2ch, rep from first * to last 3ch sp, (1tr, 1ch, 1tr, 1ch, 1tr, 1ch, 1tr, 1ch, 1tr), 2ch, join with a sl st in first dc made.

4th round: sl st in first 3ch sp, 1dc in same 3ch sp, 3ch, 1tr in next tr, (2ch, 1tr in next tr) 6 times, 3ch, 1dc in next 3ch sp, 3ch, *1tr in next tr, (2ch, 1tr in next tr) 4 times, 3ch, 1dc in next 3ch sp, 3ch, rep from * to next corner, 1tr in next tr, (2ch, 1tr in next tr) 6 times, 3ch, 1dc in next 3ch sp, 3ch, rep from first * to end, omitting the corner, 3ch, and 1dc at end of last rep, join with a sl st in first dc.

5th round: sl st in each st to next 2ch sp, sl st in 2ch sp, 3ch, holding last loop of each tr on hook make 2tr in same 2ch sp as sl st, yoh and draw through all 3 loops on hook, *3ch, 1tr in first ch, holding last loop of each tr on hook make 3tr in next 2ch sp, yoh and draw through all 4 loops on hook, rep from * to end, 3ch, 1tr in first ch, join with a sl st in top of 3ch made at beg.
Fasten off.
Fill cushion with insert. Sew up the opening.

ROSE TRIM

Make 6ch, join with a sl st in first ch to form a ring.
1st round: 6ch, *1tr in the ring, 3ch, rep from * 6 times, join with a sl st in 3rd of 6ch made at beg (there should be eight spaces).
2nd round: 1ch, *(1dc, 1tr, 3dtr, 1tr, 1dc) in next 3ch sp, rep from * to end, join with a sl st in 1ch made at beg (eight petals).
3rd round: 1dc in same place as sl st, (keeping chain at back of work), 5ch, *miss (1dc, 1tr, 3dtr, 1tr, 1dc), 1dc in sp before next dc, (keeping chain at the back of work), 5ch, rep from * to end, join with a sl st in first dc.
4th round: 1ch, *(1dc, 2tr, 3dtr, 2tr, 1dc) in next 5ch loop, rep from * to end, join with a sl st in first ch.
5th round: 1dc in same place as sl st, (keeping chain at back of work), 7ch, *miss (1dc, 2tr, 3dtr, 2tr, 1dc), 1dc in sp before next dc, (keeping chain at back of work), 7ch, rep from * to end. join with a sl st in first dc.
6th round: 1ch, *(1dc, 3tr, 3dtr, 3tr, 1dc) in next 7ch loop, rep from * to end, join with a sl st in first ch.
Fasten off. Sew to cushion in top right hand corner.

ROUND CUSHION

Materials

2 circles of fabric each 42 cm (16½") in diameter to fit a 40 cm (16") round cushion insert

30 g DMC Maeva No 10 crochet cotton

1.75 mm crochet hook, or hook that will work through two thicknesses of fabric with ease

Right sides together, sew two circles of fabric together, leaving an opening for the cushion insert. Turn right sides out.

If the fabric is too thick for the hook to go through you may have to get it hemstitched, making sure that you leave an opening for the cushion insert.

Note: Work both pieces of material together.

1st round: Starting past the opening, insert hook through both thicknesses of fabric, yoh and draw yarn through, make 1ch (this will be the first dc), work dc evenly in multiples of 12 to the opening, then continue to work through only one thickness of fabric with dc in multiples of 12 to end, join with a sl st in first dc. (You may have to work 2dc in same place to end up with the number required.)

2nd round: (3ch, 1tr, 3ch, 2tr) in same place as sl st, 3ch, miss 2dc, 1dc in each of next 7dc, *3ch, miss 2dc, (2tr, 3ch, 2tr) in next dc, 3ch, miss 2dc, 1dc in each of next 7dc, rep from * to last 2dc, 3ch, miss 2dc, join with a sl st in top of 3ch made at beg.

3rd round: 3ch, 1tr in next tr (2tr, 3ch, 2tr) in next 3ch sp, 1tr in each of next 2tr, (3ch, miss 1dc, 1dc in next dc) 3 times, 3ch, *1tr in each of next 2tr, (2tr, 3ch, 2tr) in next 3ch sp, 1tr in each of next 2tr, (3ch, miss 1dc, 1dc in next dc) 3 times, 3ch, rep from * to end, join with a sl st in top of 3ch made at beg.

4th round: 3ch, 1tr in each of next 3tr, (2tr, 3ch, 2tr) in next 3ch sp, 1tr in each of next 4tr, 3ch, miss next 3ch sp, 1dc in next 3ch sp, 3ch, 1dc in next 3ch sp, 3ch, *1tr in each of next 4tr, (2tr, 3ch, 2tr) in next 3ch sp, 1tr in each of next 4tr, 3ch, miss next 3ch sp, 1dc in next 3ch sp, 3ch, 1dc in next 3ch sp, 3ch, rep from * to end, join with a sl st in top of 3ch made at beg.

5th round: 3ch, 1tr in each of next 5tr, (3tr, 3ch, sl st in top of last tr, 2tr) in next 3ch sp, 1tr in each of next 6tr, 3ch, miss next 3ch sp, 1dc in next 3ch sp, 3ch, *1tr in each of next 6tr, (3tr, 3ch, sl st in top of last tr, 2tr) in next 3ch sp, 1tr in each

of next 6tr, 3ch, miss next 3ch sp, 1dc in next 3ch sp, 3ch, rep from * to end, join with a sl st in top of 3ch made at beg.
Fasten off.

FLOWER TRIM

Make 10ch, join with a sl st in first ch made to form a ring.
1st round: 1ch, (3dc in ring, 20ch) 6 times, join with a sl st in first dc.
2nd round: Miss same dc as sl st, 1dc in next dc, *(1dc, 1htr, 10tr, 3ch, sl st in last tr, 10tr, 1htr, 1dc) in 20ch loop, miss 1dc, 1dc in next dc, rep from * to end omitting dc at end of last rep, join with a sl st in first dc.
Fasten off. Sew to centre of cushion.
Put cushion insert in the opening, and sew up opening.

INDEX